Rhetoric: A Very Short Introduction

VERY SHORT INTRODUCTIONS are for anyone wanting a stimulating and accessible way into a new subject. They are written by experts, and have been translated into more than 45 different languages.

The series began in 1995, and now covers a wide variety of topics in every discipline. The VSI library now contains over 500 volumes—a Very Short Introduction to everything from Psychology and Philosophy of Science to American History and Relativity—and continues to grow in every subject area.

Titles in the series include the following:

Richard Toye

RHETORIC

A Very Short Introduction

OXFORD
UNIVERSITY PRESS

Great Clarendon Street, Oxford, OX2 6DP,
United Kingdom

Oxford University Press is a department of the University of Oxford.
It furthers the University's objective of excellence in research, scholarship,
and education by publishing worldwide. Oxford is a registered trade mark of
Oxford University Press in the UK and in certain other countries

British Library Cataloguing in Publication Data
Data available

ISBN 978-0-19-965136-8

Printed and bound by
CPI Group (UK) Ltd, Croydon, CR0 4YY

Contents

Acknowledgements

I am grateful to numerous friends and colleagues who have made suggestions or who have read drafts and offered comments. They are: Simon Barton, Jeremy Black, Julia Crick, Henry French, Maria Fusaro, Chris Gill, Sarah Hamilton, David Horrell, Justin Jones, James Mark, Richard Overy, Tim Rees, Matthew Rendle, Martin Thomas, and Arjan Zuiderhoek. Any errors that remain are of course my own.

I am grateful to Andrea Keegan, Luciana O'Flaherty, Emma Marchant, and Erica Martin at OUP. Joy Mellor did the copyediting. I would also like to thank my agent, Natasha Fairweather of A. P. Watt, and her assistant, Donald Winchester.

Stephen Collins very kindly facilitated the reproduction of his excellent Churchill cartoon.

Finally, I would like to thank Kristine Vaaler, who read the typescript and made valuable suggestions, and our sons, Sven and Tristan, who were excused on grounds of youth.

This book is dedicated to Mark and Themis Stringer, in celebration of twenty years of friendship.

List of illustrations

Introduction

Victor Klemperer was a brilliant scholar of language born to a German-Jewish family in 1881 and later baptized as a Christian. After Hitler came to power, Klemperer began to document the regime's tyranny in his extensive diary. The Nazis forced him out of his university position in 1935. The fact that he was married to a non-Jew allowed him to survive, in miserable conditions, much longer than would otherwise have been possible; but early in 1945 he was selected for deportation, which meant death. However, the Allied bombing raid on Dresden in February facilitated his escape. Remarkably, not only did Klemperer and his wife survive the war, but so did his diary, and he later drew on it in his classic study of the language of the Third Reich. This noted how 'Nazism permeated the flesh and blood of the people through single words, idioms and sentence structures which were imposed on them in a million repetitions and taken on board mechanically and unconsciously.' But although he despised Nazi rhetoric, Klemperer did not think it could merely be dismissed and forgotten. As he put it, 'what a man says may be a pack of lies—but his true self is laid bare for all to see in the style of his utterances.'

Society's attitudes to rhetoric are often very negative. It is usually seen as a synonym for shallow, deceptive language—the opposite of 'substance'. In this, we can still see the influence of Plato, who launched a powerful assault on rhetoric as the enemy of logical discourse. Undeniably, there are many who, like the Nazis, use it self-servingly, promoting irrationality and enmity. But Klemperer's point was an important one. Even in the extreme case of totalitarian hate-speech, rhetoric is not something that can be treated simply as a surface phenomenon and ignored. Language is a kind of ideological fingerprint which—if only we know how to interpret it—gives its author away, even as he or she attempts to dissemble. We therefore need to see *into* rhetoric rather than *beyond* it. We further need to be alive to the pertinent silences—the omissions and unmentionables—that surround even the loudest controversies and the most vocal speakers. As the psychiatrist says to his patient in T. S. Eliot's play *The Cocktail Party*:

> I learn a good deal by merely observing you,
> And letting you talk as long as you please,
> And taking note of what you do not say.

Doing all this requires us to overcome some prejudices and preconceptions. I teach a university course on modern political rhetoric. The first year it ran, I asked the group if they had experience of making debating speeches. 'Yes,' said one student, 'But I only used ordinary arguments. I didn't use any *rhetoric*.' The disdain in his voice as he uttered the word spoke volumes about the way that society views rhetoric today. I work in Britain; one would be more likely to encounter a positive view of the topic in the USA, where degree programmes in rhetoric and communication are common.

My student may have thought that he could make a speech without using it, but if rhetoric is defined (in the most basic terms) as the art of persuasion, then 'ordinary arguments' must necessarily involve it if they are to have the least chance of success. There are very good reasons for valuing the successful practice of rhetoric—who, after all, would want to be defended by a lawyer who had a perfect, logical grasp of the case but who was incapable of winning over the jury?

Furthermore, although we are accustomed to thinking of rhetoric as a public phenomenon—and indeed that is the primary focus of this book—it is also a private one. All of us project our personalities outwards in some way, visually, verbally, and even virtually (through social networking websites). Just as politicians position themselves with voters, we position ourselves in relation to a peer group (real or imagined), with rhetorical inflections of which we are frequently unconscious. Domestic arguments, as much as political ones, are suffused with claims about the past ('I did the chores last week; now it's your turn'), appeals to abstract justice ('It's not *fair*!'), and the negative characterization of opponents ('You're shirking again, as usual!'). We gain our sense of how to speak and write from the examples that surround us—those provided by the books and newspapers we read, by the politicians and presenters we see on TV, by the preachers we hear, as well as by our friends, family, and colleagues. The dividing line between the public and the private sphere is more blurred than one might assume. Naturally, a conversation has a very different dynamic to a speech, but a broadcast media interview adapts and makes use of the conventions that govern our private interactions. The supposedly private personal characteristics of politicians are often exploited by them in public in order to galvanize political action. Personal rhetoric, then, forms an important basis of individual social identities, which in turn form the grounding for political and public language.

Whether we realize it or not, then, all of us are forced to engage with rhetoric at some level, even if we shun opportunities to listen to speeches and never speak in public ourselves. This book is not intended as a defence of rhetoric—that task has been performed ably by others—and certainly not as a defence of all the ways that it is currently used. There is no virtue in ignoring the fact that we are constantly surrounded by uses of rhetoric to achieve ignoble or foolish ends, or to mask the ignorance of the speaker or writer. However, the book does take the positive case for rhetoric seriously. This case rests on the idea that rhetoric is a foundation-stone of civil society and an essential part of the democratic process. In order to function, that process requires the deployment of persuasive public speech, which in turn can serve a constructive use in promoting trust and social cohesion. If this is so, all citizens will benefit from an understanding of how rhetoric functions, in the hands of the virtuous as well as the wicked, if they are to make sense of the messages with which they are constantly bombarded. This book (which focuses mainly on the Western rhetorical tradition) introduces readers to the tools they need both to develop a critical appreciation of the rhetoric of others and—if they so wish—to improve their own rhetorical skills.

The term 'rhetoric' may properly be taken to encompass writing as well as speech (oratory). The latter is the main, but not exclusive, focus here. After all, speeches are often based on written texts and may sometimes be read in print form by many more people than actually hear them in person. The spoken word, though, does have its own particular interest, deriving partly from the theatre that surrounds it. Rhetoric cannot be conceived purely in terms of text and language, separate from the technical means by which it is conveyed to listeners and readers. In addition to textual analysis, we need to consider how the 'symbolic ritual dimension of politics' (a term used by the political scientists Alan Finlayson and James Martin) affects what rhetorical messages are produced and how they are received. The underlying premise of this book is that the 'meaning' of a given set of words cannot be derived purely from an analysis of the text, in isolation from an examination of the circumstances in which that text was delivered, mediated, and received. A work on rhetoric that focused on language and ideas to the exclusion of drama, physicality, and technology would not be sufficient to give an understanding its functions.

Although it happens that I am a historian by training, this book is not primarily a history of rhetoric. The approach is interdisciplinary, employing concepts that derive from rhetorical studies, linguistics, political science, and literary theory. The book is, however, historically informed—that is to say, rhetoric is treated as something that can only be fully understood if language is placed in its social, political, and cultural context. This implies a degree of scepticism about the idea that there are such things as immutable rhetorical laws. Whereas certain techniques, such as three point lists ('I came, I saw, I conquered'), have undoubtedly been perceived as highly effective combinations over the course of millennia, it is unclear whether this reflects an innate property of the human brain or simply a longstanding cultural persistence. And excess faith in the existence of rhetorical laws may lead the critic to overlook other factors affecting rhetorical success or failure.

In particular, it is important to be sensitive to differences in political systems—giving a speech in the British House of Commons is a different affair from giving one in the US Senate, the European Parliament, or the French National Assembly. Even apparently similar systems can produce remarkably different cultures of speech: like the British, the Australians operate the 'Westminster model' but have a tradition of robust political insult that puts the efforts of the mother country's parliamentarians in the shade. It is also important to be sensitive to change over time. In the late nineteenth century, the lengthy and convoluted orations of British Prime Minister W. E. Gladstone were widely acclaimed and sustained his enthusiastic popular following; a century later they would have seemed radically out of place.

Above all, we need to appreciate that rhetoric is not merely the means by which ideas are *expressed*, it is also a means by which they are *generated*. By this I mean that the process of debate forces rhetors (a word I shall sometimes use in place of 'speakers and writers') to articulate positions which, although they may believe that they have always held them, may in fact be quite novel. And familiar thoughts, spoken in a new context, may take on new meanings. The requirement to take a stand, and to interact with the rhetoric of both supporters and opponents, not only crystallizes ideas but also creates new ways of thinking as well as speaking. Therefore, we cannot see rhetoric *either* as an uncomplicated series of statements about the already existing opinions of its authors *or* as a mere surface phenomenon that overlies—or attempts to cover up—the 'real beliefs' that supposedly lie behind it. This has important consequences for how each of us views our relationship to the world. We may not have as much control over what we say—or how we say it—as we would like to think. Even in conditions much freer than the ones Klemperer had to face, the dominant rhetorical culture not only influences what we say in public but even infiltrates our private thoughts. Then, when we take the opportunity to 'say what we think', that culture is often reinforced in turn.

Chapter 1 gives an overview of the history of rhetoric from classical times to the late nineteenth century. Chapter 2 describes what Winston Churchill referred to as 'the scaffolding of rhetoric'—key rhetorical methods, well known in the ancient world and still used widely today. Chapter 3 addresses some fundamental questions about how the study and practice of rhetoric should be approached. Chapter 4 examines modern rhetorical phenomena in the light of the theoretical issues outlined earlier in the book. There are also brief rhetorical exercises which can be used either in the classroom or as the basis for 'thought experiments' by individual readers.

'*Language of the Third Reich*: When he spoke to youth in Nürnberg, Hitler also said: "You sing songs together." Everything is aimed at deafening the individual in collectivism.—In general pay attention to the role of *radio*! Not like other technical achievements: new contents, new philosophy. But: new *style*. Printed matter suppressed. *Oratorical*, oral. Primitive—at a higher level.'

(Victor Klemperer makes notes on Nazi rhetoric in his diary, 14 September 1934)

Chapter 1
From the Greeks to Gladstone

The idea of rhetoric as a distinct branch of knowledge had its origins in Athens in the second half of the fifth century BCE. The innovators were a group of teachers known as the Sophists, who came from different parts of Greece. Protagoras, Gorgias, Prodicus, Hippias, and Thrasymachus are the key figures remembered today; the Sicilians, Corax and Tisias, were their predecessors. We know very little of them. Their work survives only in fragments quoted by other writers. Crucially, the most systematic account of their thinking is to be found in the writings of their opponents. Therefore, in spite of the patient work of latter-day scholars, the picture is inevitably biased against them. This explains why today the word 'sophistry' acts as a shorthand for ingenious but misleading reasoning, the art of putting a bad case persuasively. Yet they deserve to be taken seriously, not least as the progenitors of a very modern notion: that the art of communication can be taught and that it is a marketable skill.

The Sophists did not invent public speaking, accounts of which can be found in earlier Greek literature (for example, by Homer), and which was already a feature of politics and the legal system. They were, however, the first self-styled knowledge professionals, who charged for their services and claimed to be able to teach the secrets of success—and not in the field of rhetoric alone. They were, in fact, offering a complete intellectual training, and their message was at the same time extremely exciting and potentially scandalous. This is why they attracted both high fees and sharp criticism. Their belief that virtue could be taught offered a meritocratic challenge to the aristocratic view that excellence was innate, transmitted by heredity and reinforced by upbringing. Athens had emerged victorious from the Persian Wars as the leading Greek state and now, as both a democracy and an empire, was struggling with her new role. In these conditions, the claim that oratory had set rules that anyone could learn—provided they had the money—was only one part of a socially provocative agenda. The Sophists called all established values into question. There were no immutable, heaven-sent laws—the only thing that counted was human experience. Their influence was important in disciplines beyond rhetoric itself. For example, the well-known historian Thucydides is often supposed to have been influenced by Sophists. His *History of the Peloponnesian War*, the foundation point of evidence-based history, placed speechmaking at the heart of the narrative, albeit the speeches were imaginative reconstructions in which the author made the speakers 'say what, in my opinion, was called for by each situation.' In common with the Sophists, he was not afraid to identify corrupt or debased rhetoric when he found examples.

The pragmatism and scepticism of the Sophists inevitably met a backlash. 'The Sophists speak and write to deceive people for their own profit', argued Xenophon. In *The Clouds* the comic playwright Aristophanes portrayed them—under the guise of the

'To fit in with the change of events, words too, had to change their usual meanings. What used to be described as a thoughtless act of aggression was now regarded as the courage one would expect to find in a party member; to think of the future and wait was merely another way of saying that one was a coward; any idea of moderation was just an attempt to disguise one's unmanly character; ability to understand a question from all sides meant that one was totally unfitted for action.'

(Thucydides describes the linguistic consequences of the civil war in Corcyra)

character of Socrates, who serves as an 'umbrella' in the play for different types of intellectual—as offering to teach how to make an 'Inferior Argument' defeat a 'Superior Argument'. (The protagonist is desperate to learn this technique so that he can avoid paying his debts, but he is caught on his own petard when his own son uses it to justify beating him.) In particular, they were accused of favouring arguments based on probability over those based on truth. The classic example is attributed to Tisias or Corax: if a brave but feeble man assaults a strong but cowardly one, he should defend himself by arguing that it was not *likely* that a weak person would attack someone strong. However, it does not seem that the Sophists prized probability arguments above all others—they were simply one tool that could be used when, as so often, the truth was inaccessible. The charges of quackery and disregard for truth may have been unfair, but they were amplified and put into a powerful form by the Sophists' most searing critic: Plato.

Plato's hostility to the Sophists had a number of bases. In two dialogues, he pitted Socrates against the Sophist Protagoras. In the *Protagoras*, the latter is portrayed as an advocate of the idea of virtues as based on communal life and shared values. In the *Theaetetus*, Protagoras is portrayed as an extreme relativist, with respect to both ethics and knowledge. Socrates—who serves as the main vehicle for Plato's ideas—is by contrast presented in both dialogues as arguing that knowledge must be based on properly conducted dialectical method. In other Platonic dialogues, such as the *Republic*, we find the idea that objective, absolute knowledge can only be obtained through dialectic. So Plato was likely profoundly opposed to the relativist conceptions of morality he linked with Protagoras. More broadly, Plato may have been critical of the Sophists, including Protagoras, because of the connections between their work and Athenian democracy, of which he was profoundly suspicious on various grounds, not least because of their trial and execution of the historical Socrates in 399 BCE.

His attack on rhetoric found its fullest expression in the *Gorgias*, a dialogue in which Plato's quasi-fictional version of Socrates presents not only rhetoric but public politics as a whole as morally suspect. They are counter-posed to philosophy and Socrates' preferred technique of dialectic—the self-improving quest for truth through logical argument between individuals. Early on, Socrates traps Gorgias into a devastating admission:

SOCRATES: It turns out, then, that rhetoric is an agent of the kind of persuasion which is designed to produce conviction, but not to educate people, about matters of right and wrong.

GORGIAS: Yes.

SOCRATES: A rhetorician, then, isn't concerned to educate the people assembled in lawcourts and so on about right and wrong; all he wants to do is persuade them. I mean, I shouldn't think it's possible for him to get so many people to understand such important matters in such a short time.

GORGIAS: No, that's right.

Gorgias quickly retires from the field and the argument is taken up first by his pupil Polus and then by Callicles (a politician who is presented as influenced by Sophists) who, however, are no better able than Gorgias is to put up a convincing defence. Socrates argues that rhetoric is not a *technē* (craft/art) but merely a knack. It is a form of superficial 'flattery' comparable to cookery, which teaches what is pleasurable rather than what is actually good for you. He claims that by contrast with the Sophists and almost all other Athenians, only he, Socrates, practises true political statesmanship: 'moral improvement rather than gratification and pleasure is always the reason for my saying anything'. It would even be better to remain silent in the face of an unjust prosecution than to demean oneself by appealing to the mob. (The historical Socrates did speak at his trial, but in a strikingly defiant manner.) Socrates does in fact admit the theoretical possibility of a noble type of rhetoric aimed at improving the souls of the citizenry, but he denies that any orator, living or dead, had ever actually practiced this form. Indeed, he presents himself as the one true exponent of the art of politics, and represents dialectic as the only proper method of argument and the only valid medium for political life.

Socrates wins his case easily—too easily. As so often in Plato's dialogues, the hero's opponents make silly mistakes, miss obvious points, and end up weakly agreeing with Socrates' suggestions, no matter how contentious. For example, Socrates condemns the statesmanship of Pericles because, although he was initially popular, towards the end of his life the ungrateful Athenians put him on trial and convicted him: therefore it is clear that his rhetoric, which should have aimed at taming the masses, had only made them wilder. None of Socrates' opponents point out the possibility of other explanations for his downfall, or suggest that even the most virtuous orator might fall victim to circumstance. Equally, there is a tension between Socrates' claim to be 'no politician' and the sophisticated rhetorical techniques that Socrates himself uses—he makes long speeches, blaming the inconsistency on his opponents' failure to argue properly. The deeper irony, of course, was that Plato used the literary-rhetorical dialogic form to disguise weaknesses in his argument and stack the cards against his enemies, the Sophists.

It is certainly true that, as Brian Vickers has argued, 'Plato's travesty of rhetoric' has been highly influential, and that the reputation of the Sophists 'has never recovered from the drubbing Plato gave it'. At the same time, it is clear that Plato would not have been able to achieve this influence had he not tapped into a deep fear, widely shared, about the irrationality of crowds and the abuse of public language. He may have been unfair in his treatment of the original Sophists, but he was surely not wrong to be concerned about the specious use of language by politicians and lawyers. In denouncing *all* rhetoric, at least in the

11

Gorgias, he overshot the mark, and the idea that human discourse on important issues could be conducted exclusively through the rarefied process of dialectic was obviously impractical. His telling allegation that rhetoric created 'belief without knowledge' echoes to this day. However, although he was able to fuel suspicion of rhetoric, he was powerless to stop the flow. The Athenian statesman Demosthenes (384–322 BCE) was perhaps the greatest of the Greek orators, and his tirades against Philip II of Macedon gave the name to a particular kind of denunciatory speech, the 'philippic', although Philip prevailed over Athens nonetheless.

'The available means of persuasion'

The relationship between dialectic and rhetoric remained controversial, even as methods of rhetorical education became more sophisticated. Isocrates (436–338 BCE) was one of the renowned 'ten Attic orators', some of whom wrote speeches for other people. The school of rhetoric he founded maintained the now-established concentration on rhetorical rules, practice, and the use of examples. Isocrates also allowed his pupils to criticize his own draft speeches. Although he wrote a work called *Against the Sophists*, he was a Sophist himself; his target was the inferior methods of other teachers, and he may have had in view the Plato school's narrow focus on dialectic. He made a connection between rhetoric and the logic of the inner mind:

> the same arguments which we use in persuading others when we speak in public, we employ also when we deliberate in our own thoughts; and, while we call eloquent those who are able to speak before a crowd, we regard as sage those who most skilfully debate their problems in their own minds.

His position was based on a form of intellectual humility. As it was impossible for the human mind to ascertain scientifically what should be said or done, wisdom lay in the use of conjecture to reach, as far as possible the best course of action—hence the need for rhetorical deliberation to establish the way forward.

Aristotle (384–322 BCE) also offered a defence of rhetoric, but a less holistic one. He was a pupil of Plato, but one whose ideas were often very different from Plato's, and one of his early works, now lost except in fragments, may have been an attack on Isocrates and a defence of the claim that rhetoric was not a *techne*. However, the writings that we now know as the *Art of Rhetoric*—its three books may not have been intended as a single work—explicitly views it as such. Its first sentence is 'Rhetoric is the counterpart of dialectic' which both puts the two on an equal footing and recognizes them as separate. In Aristotle's view, not everyone was capable of following formal logic. It was therefore necessary to use, when attempting to persuade people, concepts that were available to everyone. Moreover, if rhetoric could indeed be put to wrong use, this was true of 'all good things except excellence', including strength, health, wealth, and strategic skill. The capacity to make contradictory cases was needed, not so that it could be used to persuade men to do evil, but in order that one could recognize and refute unjust arguments. Rhetoric was a tool of self-defence using reason—as legitimate as the use of the body for the same purpose, and more particularly human.

Aristotle advanced a range of important definitions. Rhetoric itself was 'the faculty of observing in any given case the available means of persuasion'. That is to say, it was not simply about creating beautiful phrases, but about reading situations and seeing how elements of them could be deployed most effectively in order to win over an audience (and about reading the specific audience to see what will work with *them*.) He also distinguished between three genres: forensic (or courtroom) rhetoric; epideictic (or display) rhetoric, such as a funeral oration; and deliberative rhetoric, which attempts to persuade the audience to a specific course of action (such as passing a piece of legislation or declaring war). He further distinguished between three types of 'proof' that a speech might contain: 'The first kind depends on the personal character of the speaker; the second on putting the audience into a certain frame of mind; the third on the proof, or the apparent proof, provided by the words of the speech itself.' These are the appeals to *ēthos* (character), *pathos* (emotion, or the emotional character of the audience), and *logos* (logic or discourse). Aristotle seemed here to be trying to have it both ways. By insisting that rhetoric dealt with proof, he emphasized its dependence on reason rather than emotion. At the same time, by claiming that *ēthos* and *pathos* were themselves varieties of proof, he elevated potentially manipulative techniques to a similar status as logic. But in spite of its inconsistencies, Aristotle's treatise was a remarkable effort to deal systematically with the problem of rhetoric, and the categorization he devised was to have a long influence.

Exercise

You and your friends are embarked on a perilous jungle adventure. Suddenly the group's leader, Geraldine, urges you all to jump into a nearby lake. 'Comrades,' she says, 'the danger is terrible, and I have no time to explain. But I have not let you down in the past, so trust me please and save yourselves now. Jump, comrades, jump!'

Nigel, another member of the group, replies: 'Calm, my friends. It is true that Geraldine is, in general, a wise leader, and she has saved our lives many times before. However, you will remember from past experience that she also has a great love of cruel practical jokes. There is no evident threat and I note that she is not jumping herself. Ignore her, friends, or you will get soggy for no reason!'

Use *this example as the starting point for a discussion of whether the character of a speaker can affect the validity of their argument. Compose a third speech by a further member of the group embodying your conclusions.*

Greek knowledge, Roman values

In the period after Aristotle's death, rhetorical study became an increasingly essential part of upper class young men's education. Their studies would include the *progymnasmata*—a series of basic rhetorical exercises—as well more advanced forms of practice and explorations of theory. Most of the many rhetorical handbooks produced by Aristotle's Peripatetic School are now lost, but its teachings were to be influential in Rome; also in circulation were the ideas of the Stoic School, which taught a brief and austere style of speech. However, it would be misleading to imagine that there was a timeless 'classical tradition' of rhetoric that transferred itself seamlessly from the Greeks to the Romans, independent of the impact of time, culture, and location. Greek learning was not a uniform body of knowledge but the product of heterogeneous contributions; and its reception in Rome was highly contested. Even those who welcomed it were quite capable of taking Greek authors out of context and using them for their own purposes. Thus Hellenistic rhetorical teaching was not taken over wholesale but rather selectively appropriated and domesticated. The field of rhetoric was a construct that reflected, maintained, and shaped established social norms. As Gualtiero Calboli and William J. Dominik suggest, 'Roman rhetoric is best viewed as part of a larger cultural process, that is, not just as a system of rules applicable to spoken and written language but as a fundamental component in the exploration of Roman society and literature.' Rhetoric was not just a means of argumentation; it was something that was *argued about*, and was controversial precisely because of this link to wider values.

The exact routes and timings of the transmission of Greek rhetorical theory are unclear. The first firm date is 161 BCE, when an edict—probably ineffective—ordered the expulsion of Greek teachers of rhetoric from Rome. The influence of Greece was later described by Marcus Tullius Cicero (106–43 BCE), who was himself an extremely effective orator, both as a lawyer and as a politician, as well as being a historian and theorist of rhetoric. The evidence for Cicero's life and thinking is abundant, whereas for many other figures it is sparse. It is therefore difficult to avoid looking at Roman rhetoric—or at least that of his predecessors—through the eyes of this quintessential figure. According to Cicero, early Roman orators were capable of untutored brilliance, but they lacked the style and urbanity that acquaintance with Greek teachings could provide. Equipped with this knowledge, the Roman people became 'fired with a really incredible enthusiasm for eloquence' and outstripped all other races in their skill at it. However, this should not be seen as a neutral observation but rather as a vindication of his own polished style against critics who condemned it as decadent. After his murder during the convulsions that followed the assassination of Julius Caesar, Cicero's oratory was to achieve iconic status. This owed something both to his efforts during his lifetime to secure his own rhetorical reputation and to the political purposes that his posthumous 'canonization' as the supposedly ideal orator served for others.

In Cicero's world, the Republican political elite used oratory at public meetings as a means to boost their power by generating evidence of popular support. And in contrast to the Athenian public assembly, where all male citizens could speak, Senate rhetoric was the preserve of the propertied. Linguistic culture, then, was linked to the social order. Rhetorical exercises included forms of role-playing that allowed Roman adolescents to inhabit and practice the positions of authority—lawyer, slave-holder, patron—for which they were being prepared. Ideas about rhetoric and public speaking, indeed, have never been socially neutral but have always had connections to hierarchies and tensions within society.

If rhetoric was about class, it was also about gender. Public speaking was an exclusively male activity, but the technique of artful persuasion—in contrast to 'action'—had unwelcome connotations of feminine wiliness for the Romans. (Notwithstanding their literary

The power of Cicero's rhetoric

'So also it is related that when Quintus Ligarius was prosecuted for having been in arms against Caesar, and Cicero had undertaken his defence, Caesar said to his friends, "Why might we not as well once more hear a speech from Cicero? Ligarius, there is no question, is a wicked man and an enemy." But when Cicero began to speak, he wonderfully moved him, and proceeded in his speech with such varied *pathos*, and such a charm of language, that the colour of Caesar's countenance often changed, and it was evident that all the passions of his soul were in commotion. At length, the orator touching upon the Pharsalian battle, he was so affected that his body trembled, and some of the papers he held dropped out of his hands. And thus he was overpowered, and acquitted Ligarius.'

(From Plutarch's *Life of Cicero*)

capacity, as seen in the work of the poet Sappho, women themselves were all but completely marginalized in classical rhetoric.) Orators therefore worked hard to assert their manliness—and hence their fitness to rule—through erect posture, firm but controlled gesture, and a tone of voice that avoided high-pitched 'womanish screeching'. Literal uprightness was an expression of moral uprightness and masculinity. If the physical showmanship was a form of political theatre, then speeches were also literary products, in a world where the boundaries between rhetoric, history, and literature were extremely fuzzy. The work of Rome's poets and satirists often reflected their own rhetorical training. Speeches were often written down, copied, and circulated after delivery, perhaps as much for aesthetic appreciation as for more concrete purposes. This required a workforce, the slaves and freedmen known as *literati*, and the beginnings of a technology: Cicero's slave Tiro has been credited with the invention of a form of shorthand that allowed speeches to be transcribed verbatim.

The performance and reception of rhetoric was affected by Senate rules of precedence and by courtroom procedures and customs (which included advocates hiring audience members to applaud them). It was also influenced by broader political structures. After the fall of the Republic, many contemporaries detected a decline in rhetorical standards. However, such claims must be treated cautiously, as they often operated as part of wider social and political critiques. There were still plenty of opportunities to practice oratory under the Empire, although political rhetoric increasingly tended towards flattering the emperors through panegyric (speeches of uncritical praise). There remained a vibrant culture of rhetorical learning. Marcus Fabius Quintilianus (c. 35–c. 96 CE), known to us as Quintilian, wrote a landmark twelve volume treatise which treated rhetoric as an ethical discipline and venerated Cicero. Greek rhetorical culture also found new expression within the Roman Empire through the so-called Second Sophistic of the second and third centuries, although the ways in which this movement was discussed by contemporaries helped reinforce the image of Sophism as the triumph of style over substance.

Survival and adaptation during the Middle Ages

There is a popular belief that classical learning died out during the so-called 'Dark Ages' (a term medievalists no longer use) only to be revived, more or less spontaneously, during the later medieval period and thereafter. Certainly, many works, including important works on rhetoric, disappeared or were forgotten for a long time. However, more rhetorical texts may have circulated in this period than was once thought. Moreover, the influence of Greek and Roman rhetoric can be found in early Christian writings, including the Bible. St. Paul was born a Roman citizen, and whether or not he had formal training in rhetoric, his letters demonstrate argumentative techniques that reflect culturally established rhetorical norms. (These letters were, in fact, designed to be read out at Christian assemblies, and were thus an interesting hybrid rhetorical form.) Later, St. Augustine's discussion of the methods appropriate for a Christian speaker owed much to Cicero and Quintilian. St. Jerome, in a vision, heard himself accused of being 'not a Christian, but a Ciceronian'. Christians might have been suspicious of rhetoric as a pagan or secular discipline, but if they wanted to win converts they could hardly ignore its techniques. It was also hard for later writers to avoid an interest in works that had been so fascinating to the Church Fathers.

We should not, however, treat classical learning or indeed rhetoric itself as though it were Western property. Forms of oratory existed in many if not all societies: for example, a system of rhetoric had developed in China in the fifth to third centuries BCE, separately to Greek rhetoric but with some features in common with it. Roman control of the region we now know as the Middle East left a strong rhetorical legacy, and not only for Christians. The birth of Islam during the seventh century CE saw the continuation of earlier cultural phenomena, adapted to new purposes and conditions. Philip Halldén has argued that 'In the field of rhetoric, it meant that the old traditions came to be adapted to the special needs of Muslim preachers, just as the ancient tradition of pagan rhetoric had been adapted for Christian purposes.' Whether Islamic preaching manuals were modelled on earlier rhetorical handbooks is unclear, but the Arabic world was an important repository of classical learning, and in due course some of it was projected back to Europe, perhaps partly via the Byzantine Empire and Spain. Thus, Aristotle's *Art of Rhetoric* owed its eventual reintroduction to Europe to its translation into Latin from Arabic. But regardless of the influences on it, Islamic rhetoric must be understood in its own terms. The word 'rhetoric' itself can be translated into Arabic in two ways. *Fann al-khatāba* relates to the skill of religious preaching to lay people, with an emphasis on expression and the rendering of ideas. *Ilm al-balāgha*—the 'science of eloquence'— relates to linguistic purity. *Ilm al-balāgha* had religious as well as literary implications. As Islam expanded, it often came into contact with non-Arabic cultures. As Arabic was the language of religious transmission there was a strong concern with keeping it 'clean' or 'pristine'—not that it could always be agreed precisely what that meant.

The interface between the Christian and Muslim worlds was often violent, and rhetoric played its part in stoking conflict. One of the most famous speeches of the middle ages was made by Pope Urban II at Clermont in 1095, launching the First Crusade that culminated in the sack of Jerusalem four years later. We do not know exactly what he said: we have four different versions of the speech, written from memory by supposed eyewitnesses after the outcome of the Crusade was known. The writers may therefore have constructed Urban's words in a way that reflected what it seemed to them retrospectively that he *ought* to have said—rather like Thucydides' technique, in fact. This habit of subordinating literal truth to moral purpose was a broader feature of medieval thinking. Understandably, it is something that many modern scholars have deplored. The condemnation has extended to the rhetorical learning of the time. Scholars such as Vickers have bemoaned the 'fragmentation' of rhetoric during the Middle Ages.

In this analysis, the art of secular speaking died. Rhetoric was subordinated to grammar and logic, the other parts of the educational curriculum (or 'trivium'). It drifted from the practical realm to the narrow intellectual one (alternatively, according to some, it suffered from an excessively practical focus). It became 'fossilized'; what survived of classical learning was wrenched out of context; and although there was a proliferation of textbooks, these became so specialized that they lost their broader purpose. The habit of writing commentaries on rhetorical and other texts signalled a mindless reverence for authority. It was only later, Vickers argues, that 'Renaissance rhetoric got things back into the proper perspective.'

There is, however, another way of looking at the same set of problems. The writing of commentaries can be seen, not as a form of slavish intellectual deference, but as a means of elucidating, and entering into a form of dialogue with, predecessors who were not always treated uncritically. Indeed, the habit of mining classical authors for whatever was of use—rather than examining them in their own terms and for their own sake—may be seen as ruthlessly utilitarian. John O. Ward has argued for the existence of a medieval 'rhetorical revolution'. This, he suggests, consisted precisely of a willingness to adapt classical theory for current purposes, by stripping away irrelevant matter through the processes of editing, compilation, and excerption. These activities 'not only produced new syntheses of local relevance, but also provided a climate in which the major classical texts would at least be sufficiently copied as to survive into Renaissance times.' If so, the Middle Ages were less a rhetorical wrong turning than a route-marker for later developments.

It is difficult to overstate the importance of rhetoric to medieval education and literature. Of course, the numbers of the literate were very small. Sophisticated forms of teaching were mainly

A medieval rhetorical education

'In view of the fact that exercise both strengthens and sharpens the mind, Bernard would bend every effort to bring his students to imitate what they were hearing. [...] He would also explain the poets and orators who were to serve as models for the boys in their introductory exercises in imitating prose and poetry. Pointing out how the diction of the authors was so skilfully connected, and what they had to say was so elegantly concluded, he would admonish his students to follow their example.'

(The methods of the twelfth century teacher Bernard of Chartres, recalled by John of Salisbury in his *Metalogicon* (1159), I. 24)

conducted in Latin and the shortage of written texts meant that memorization was important. There was an emphasis on the imitation and amplification of model texts, and a tendency to advocate rigid structural formulae. Illustrations of preachers counting on their fingers may suggest a method for marking off the sections of their sermons as they were delivered. The study of poetry encouraged the use of allegory, and the declamations practiced in the schoolroom had an impact on other forms of writing, such as histories that included representations, often clearly imaginary, of speeches and debates. When writers on factual topics included elements that appear either absurd or obviously untrue, we must not be too swift to dismiss them as credulous or deluded. These were sophisticated men writing in elaborate codes for the benefit of fellow initiates. The exact purposes of the fictive elements may be hard to grasp, but they clearly served a rhetorical purpose in pointing to perceived higher truths in a form which learned readers would have been expected to understand.

Renaissance, Enlightenment, Revolution

If the irrationalism of the Middle Ages should not be exaggerated, neither should the rationalism and 'modernity' of the Renaissance. In spite of the continuities, though, there were also dramatic technological and ideological developments that affected the way that rhetoric was disseminated and received. The invention of the printing press facilitated the widespread dissemination of texts, most famously the Bible, but also an increasing number of rhetorical handbooks written in the vernacular. The ability to distribute tracts and sermons on a large scale helped drive forward the Reformation, which in turn had consequences for the way that rhetoric was discussed. Thomas Wilson, Protestant author of the *Arte of Rhetorique*, suggested that when Jesus gave his disciples bread and said 'This is my body' this was intended as a rhetorical symbol not a literal truth. His implication was that Catholics had fallen into serious theological error through an inability to interpret the linguistic structures of the Scriptures. This was not meant to imply that Biblical symbols were not, in their own way, 'true'. Martin Luther noted that 'worldly rhetoricians boast of arranging words in such a way as to give the impression of communicating and making visible the thing itself: this is precisely the characteristic of [St.] Paul, that is to say of the Holy Spirit.'

Classical learning remained vitally important, and was at the centre of the humanist education advocated by scholars such as Erasmus. The desire to use rhetorical teaching to groom a virtuous political elite was reflected in Thomas Elyot's influential *The Book named the Governor*, amongst other works. (The advice-manual genre was brilliantly subverted in Machiavelli's *The Prince*, which urged rulers to lie to their people when so doing was necessary for the survival of the state.) English grammar schools expected their students to master the art of debating; it was probably at school that Shakespeare first encountered some of the classical sources he used in his plays. Quentin Skinner—who has shown the influence of such training on the work of the political philosopher Thomas Hobbes—has noted how the Classics were exploited for Christian purposes. He writes:

> With its techniques for exciting the emotions, the ancient *ars rhetorica* [art of rhetoric], and especially the classical Grand Style, accordingly came to be viewed as a method for expressing human spirituality, and hence as a method for illuminating and directing us towards the truth, not for deflecting us from it.

Literary rhetoric too could serve religious purposes. John Milton's classically influenced *Paradise Lost* put persuasive speeches in the mouth of the devil. This was not as an endorsement of immorality but was rather part of Milton's overall attempt to 'justify the ways of God to men'. As a later commentator noted, Milton showed Satan 'justifying all his diabolical practices with the subtleties of pretended reason' before presenting him at last 'abashed and shrinking before the awful nature of goodness'. The scientists of the era, too, were classically educated Christians, and gave considerable thought to the problem of presenting revolutionary findings persuasively, in order to avoid hostility or ridicule.

Those who studied and practiced rhetoric were as liable as anyone to be caught up in the political and religious tumult of the era. Petrus Ramus, a French rhetorician who proposed a simplified curriculum in which dialectic was separated from rhetoric, was a Protestant convert who fell victim to the St. Bartholomew's Day massacre of 1572. Milton suffered for his republican sympathies after the restoration of Charles II and was forced to delay publication of *Paradise Lost*. In the same period, Margaret Fell wrote *Women's Speaking Justified* while imprisoned for her Quaker beliefs. Fell used examples from scripture to confute those who opposed preaching by females. Although women were excluded from rhetorical education, a few, like her, began to contest their marginalization. Jane Donawerth argues that writers such as Madeleine de Scudéry and Mary Astell reinterpreted classical theory to create a legitimate sphere for female speech in the domain of conversation rather than public speaking. Consciously or otherwise, they deployed common gender stereotypes (male–public/female–private) in order to carve out a space for female rhetorical persuasion, albeit in a highly restricted context.

During the eighteenth century, the spread of newspapers and the growth of representative institutions combined with the ideology of the Enlightenment to shape the way that rhetoric was delivered and received. Classical learning remained important but, as always, it was adapted and deployed for current purposes. Indeed, those who prided themselves on being 'men of reason' felt that in some ways they had improved on the ancients' way of doing things.

The philosopher David Hume (1711–76) felt that the modern age was both 'superior in philosophy' and 'much inferior in eloquence' to the classical era. The alleged decline of eloquence, of course, is a perennial complaint, and Hume's verdict seems harsh given that this was the era of the great parliamentary speeches of William Pitt the Elder. However, the reasons that he gave for it were revealing of some widely held attitudes. First, he claimed, eloquence was now discouraged by 'the multiplicity and intricacy of laws', which were far more complex than those of Greece and Rome. A lawyer who needed to master detailed statutes and precedents would appear absurd if he instead fell back on a Ciceronian appeal to equity and good sense. Second, modern rationality militated against some of the courtroom tricks of antiquity. If someone was accused of murder, the case had to be proven with witnesses and evidence. It would be ridiculous to 'introduce the relations of the dead; and, at a signal, make them throw themselves at the feet of the judges, imploring justice with tears and lamentations'. Banishing such appeals to *pathos* from public discourse reduced speakers 'merely to modern eloquence; that is, to good sense, delivered in proper expression.' Thus, complexity and rationality had combined to render public speech increasingly mediocre. (By contrast with Hume, the economist Adam Smith suggested that commercial development improved the quality of a nation's prose, which served as the language of business.) Hume felt that orators should respond by redoubling their efforts, especially through better organization and planning of their material. He, on the whole, was making observations about society rather than complaining about it; but, in other hands, claims about the deterioration of rhetoric could serve as a vehicle for discontent about the seeming vulgarity of modern life.

Quality aside, the social importance of rhetoric was if anything increasing. As the Divine Right of Kings came under growing challenge, the new forms of government that emerged required more public deliberation—or, depending on one's point of view, more crude populism and demagogic appeal. Appeals to reason,

The perpetual complaint of rhetorical decline

'[T]he age of Rhetoric, like that of Chivalry, has passed amongst forgotten things [...] Suppose yourself an Ancient Athenian, at some customary display of Athenian oratory, what will be the topics? Peace, or war, vengeance for public wrongs, or mercy to prostrate submission, national honour and national gratitude, glory and shame, and every aspect of open appeal to the primal sensibilities of man. On the other hand, enter an English Parliament, having the most of a popular character in its constitution and practice, that is to be found in the Europe of this day; and the subject of debate will probably be a road bill, a bill for enabling a coal-gas company to assume certain privileges against a competitor in oil-gas; a bill for disfranchising a corrupt borough, or perhaps some technical point of form in the Exchequer Bills bill. So much is the face of public business vulgarized by details.'

(Thomas De Quincey, 'Rhetoric', 1828, in *De Quincey's Collected Writings*, Vol. X, pp. 97–8)

liberty, and natural law were by no means always couched in the measured, pedestrian style that Hume thought was characteristic of 'modern eloquence'—they could be inflammatory and vituperative. The French Revolution not only destroyed existing political structures; it attempted a linguistic revolution too. The revolutionaries stripped their language of Christian references (although not of all religious connotations). *Vive la Nation* supplanted *Vive le Roi*; even the names of the months were changed. Obsessed with the threat of counter-revolution and conspiracy, radicals specialized in the 'rhetoric of denunciation'. Conservatives, for their part, turned to history and familial metaphors to justify royal authority. The leaders on both sides shared a similar rhetorical education based on the classics gained in religious institutions. For example, the fanatical Maximilian de Robespierre attended Christian colleges and was his rhetoric teacher's star pupil. He went on to become a lawyer, a profession that dominated public life during the Revolution. For the revolutionaries, classical learning—notably the writings of progressive thinkers such as Rousseau and Voltaire—formed a rhetorical resource that could be put to new purposes.

A speaker in the National Assembly in Paris faced a multiplicity of audiences. These consisted not only of his fellow legislators and members of the public physically present in the gallery, but also members of the many political clubs and societies that had sprung up across France, who received commentary on proceedings from the proliferation of new periodicals. Plenty of revolutionary speeches were written in advance with publication clearly in mind. Nor was the audience purely domestic. In Britain, the Revolution triggered a battle over political language. Conservatives at last succeeded in wresting the discourse of patriotism from the radicals and reformers who had previously wielded it as a weapon against governmental corruption. They not only attacked the Revolution's ideas, they attacked the very language in which they were expressed and the techniques by which they were disseminated. In 1791, Edmund Burke denounced the revolutionaries' 'false philosophy and false rhetoric [...] calculated to captivate and influence the vulgar mind, and to excite sedition in the countries in which it is ordered to be circulated.' The fears generated by radical language were intense.

The rhetoric of mass democracy

The rhetorical consequences of the American Revolution were somewhat different. For a very long time, the US system fell far short of a full democratic franchise, but it nonetheless generated pressures that would become familiar in societies with mass electorates. Alexis de Tocqueville, French observer of *Democracy in America*, noted that members of Congress, owing their position to the voters, became unnecessarily loquacious in the hope of gratifying their constituents. (The British franchise, by contrast, was more restricted, and there were plenty of MPs who never spoke at all.) Thus, 'All laws that tend to make the representative more dependent on the elector affect not only the conduct of the legislators [...] but also their language. They exercise a simultaneous influence on affairs themselves and on the manner in which affairs are discussed.' In other words, widening the franchise changed the nature of political discourse. In spite of the downside that he identified, De Tocqueville's broad conclusion was wholly positive. In his assessment, the proceedings of the British parliament had not generated much interest abroad at any point in the last 150 years, 'whereas Europe was excited by the very first debates that took place in the small colonial assemblies of America at the time of the Revolution.' This, in his view, was because the task of speaking on behalf of a whole nation—rather than simply an aristocratic class—improved an orator's thinking and linguistic power. 'Hence the political debates of a democratic people, however small it may be, have a degree of breadth that frequently renders them attractive to mankind.'

De Tocqueville's insights into how political structures shaped rhetoric were valuable, but his comments had a naïve aspect. The passage seemed to reflect an idealistic view that social conflicts could be worked through rationally via what the English constitutional theorist Walter Bagehot later called 'government by discussion'. It ignored the lack of power of marginalized groups in society: non-whites, women, and the poor. These groups sometimes could use rhetoric as a tool of self-defence, but only under severe constraints. Oratory played an important role in collective decision-making in Native American society, but we have few texts, save those made in the context of treaty negotiations or military surrender to whites. Most of these texts were recorded by whites, and tend to reinforce the stereotype of the eloquent 'noble savage'.

Similarly, in 1851 the ex-slave Sojourner Truth made a moving address to a women's rights convention. This is generally known as the 'Aren't I a woman?' speech. However, the famous version of the speech, in which this question was posed four times, was only recorded years later—the phrase does not occur in an earlier, near contemporary account. Moreover, the famous version rendered Truth's words in a Southern dialect. In fact she had grown up in New York State, and prided herself on her 'fairly correct English'. It is hard to escape her own conclusion that well-meaning sympathizers took 'an unfair advantage of her', both by giving her the expected dialect and (one suspects) by putting words into her mouth.

Established politicians, of course, found it much easier to shape the way their rhetoric was received. W. E. Gladstone, four times British Prime Minister in the late nineteenth century, provides a notable case of skilful media management. He would have been deeply uncomfortable with many aspects of twenty-first century political conduct. Nevertheless, the so-called Midlothian Campaign of 1879–80 was a dramatic moment in the development of modern political technique, in which Gladstone scaled his way back to power through a series of excoriating speeches attacking Benjamin Disraeli's Conservative government. It was a triumph made possible by the growth of the press, which had been liberated from taxation and revolutionized by technology. The accounts telegraphed to London by shorthand writers were printed at length in newspapers that were then distributed by railway, so that the whole country could hang on the Grand Old Man's every word (see Figure 1). Gladstone was both a pillar of classical learning and a pioneer of the mass meeting in the new age of the expanded franchise—he was an orator given to long, highfalutin speeches who also developed his own cult of personality.

To his opponents, Gladstone's techniques were evidence of his rabble-rousing, demagoguery, and tendency to class warfare, but even so, they were obliged to emulate him if they wanted to be successful. By this time, politics had also shifted in a different way,

THE GENERAL ELECTION : MR. GLADSTONE ADDRESSING THE ELECTORS OF GREENWICH ON BLACKHEATH.

1. Gladstone addressing his constituents. Note the reporters in the foreground

in America as well as in Britain. At the end of the eighteenth century politicians had sold themselves to the voters primarily on the basis of character—that they were suitable persons to represent their constituents. By the time that Gladstone's career reached its highpoint, although personality remained very important, the primary appeal had moved towards policy. Andrew W. Robertson suggests that there was a change from 'laudatory' rhetoric, praising the candidate, to 'hortatory' rhetoric that exhorted or advised the voters to support a particular world-view. This latter type 'linked the audience in an immediate, emotional way to events, principles or policies, mostly real, often exaggerated, sometimes illusory.' Increasingly, the expectation was that politicians would pledge themselves to introduce detailed sets of measures; they would then be judged on the gap between promise and performance. The ideal of rhetorical deliberation by independent men of good character was now replaced by the selling of packages of policies directly to the people—although charismatic leaders were still generally required to achieve this successfully. This is the model of rhetoric that informs modern programmatic politics in the form that we now know it.

Conclusion

This chapter has shown that rhetoric is about much more than the arrangement of figures of speech to create a pleasing impression on listeners. At many times and in many places, rhetoric has been seen as a complete system of education, sufficient to prepare rulers for the task of governing—it has also been highly controversial, seen by some as a technique by which the unscrupulous can deceive the masses. It has links to literature, science, commerce, and private conversation. How it is received is conditioned by technology, culture, and power relations within society. Although some techniques seem perennially effective, there is no set of rules that by itself can guarantee success. In fact, attempts to lay down such rules are inevitably coloured by assumptions about topics such as class, gender, and race. This is why the investigation of rhetoric—and the ways it is contested—is a good starting point for understanding social and political questions more generally. A society's arguments reveal what it considers important—and also, obliquely, the issues it doesn't much want to discuss. Its arguments about *how* to argue, meanwhile, are a means to decode its social DNA.

Chapter 2
The scaffolding of rhetoric

In 1984, Max Atkinson, then an academic researcher and now a professional public speaking coach, tried a fascinating experiment. He trained Ann Brennan, an unknown woman with no previous public speaking experience, in some basic rhetorical techniques in preparation for a speech she was to deliver at the annual party conference of Britain's short-lived Social Democratic Party (SDP). On the day, her humorous, confident speech gained her a standing ovation and became the highlight of the conference. There was some synthetic media outrage when it emerged that this apparently 'ordinary' woman had in fact had professional advice and was participating in a TV documentary. Nonetheless, however slick her technique, she would never have succeeded so well had she not had an important message that resonated with her audience: Brennan's key point, which was to be justified by events, was that, unless it reached out beyond its natural constituency of middle class readers of *The Guardian* newspaper (a by-word for liberal progressivism), the SDP would fail at the ballot box. Far from being glib or artificial, as the media critics implied, the rhetorical tools that Atkinson gave Brennan helped her think through and articulate the things she wanted to say.

Atkinson's techniques were simple and had a long heritage. This chapter describes what Winston Churchill referred to as 'the scaffolding of rhetoric'—that is, key concepts familiar in the ancient world and still much in use today (even if many of the speakers who apply them are not consciously aware of doing so). Greek and Roman rhetorical scholars were obsessed with classifying the parts of speech, perhaps in the belief that labelling language would allow them to control it. An understanding of rhetoric by no means requires a familiarity with the whole gamut of rhetorical terms they devised. Not all of the distinctions they made were actually useful, and in these cases one may sympathize with Quintilian's complaint that 'these minute affectations about terms for things are pretentious labours!' However, there are good reasons for getting a grip of some of the most fundamental terms (and in some cases for supplementing them with the ideas of modern theorists). Labels are not vital in themselves, but they can give a handle on some of the wide variety of things it is possible to do with words. This in turn helps make one more sensitive to the different effects that speakers (or writers) may be attempting to achieve. That is important whether you are conducting a formal rhetorical analysis of a text or merely watching a TV interview. It is also possible, of course, to use these techniques yourself to improve your own speaking and writing.

It should always be remembered, though, that there is no 'recipe' that will infallibly produce success. Without what the Greeks called *kairos*—the opportune moment—even the most technically brilliant speech will fall flat. As Aristotle suggested, the art of rhetoric lies in identifying the opportunities presented by the situation at hand, not in the sterile combination of figures of speech for their own sake. What follows, then, is not a comprehensive system but rather a basic toolkit. It will help you spot some of the things that other rhetors might be trying to do and provides some models for things that you might like to try yourself. The chapter will also introduce the concept of visual rhetoric, showing how clothing, gesture, and the use of physical space can reinforce verbal messages.

The three branches of oratory

Following Aristotle, it is normal to distinguish between three types or branches of oratory: 1) forensic/judicial rhetoric (to be found in a courtroom or other legal context); 2) epideictic/display rhetoric, that is, rhetoric concerned with praise or blame; and 3) deliberative rhetoric (used to persuade a group, for example, of voters or legislators, towards a particular course of action). The distinctions, on the face of it, seem clear. Certainly, it is easy enough to establish if a given speech took place during a trial, in which case it will have belonged to the first type. However, consider the famous speech of Nelson Mandela at his trial by the South African authorities in 1963–4, which he concluded with a statement of his belief in democracy, freedom, and equal opportunities. 'It is an ideal which I hope to live for and to achieve,' he said, 'But if needs be, it is an ideal for which I am prepared to die.' Given the judicial setting this was clearly a forensic speech, although Mandela openly admitted his support for illegal violence and refused to plead for his life, in fact, he was almost daring the Apartheid regime to execute him. Yet the speech's broader purpose was political/deliberative, justifying Mandela's actions; as such it was aimed at an audience far beyond the courtroom, and indeed even beyond South Africa.

Similarly, epideictic rhetoric can be more than it seems. Shakespeare's *Julius Caesar* provides a classic example of how the boundaries can be blurred. Against the advice of his fellow assassin Cassius, Brutus gives his political rival Mark Antony permission to speak at his friend Caesar's funeral. Yet, as Cassius fears, Mark Antony does not deliver a standard eulogy. Indeed, he advertises at the start that 'I come to bury Caesar, not to praise him.' This, however, is disingenuous. While disclaiming all intention of stirring the crowd against the conspirators by drawing attention to the virtues of the man they had killed, he nonetheless actually does this, whilst keeping up a withering, sarcastic commentary on Brutus's honour. The people take the hint and revolt against Caesar's enemies: it is the turning point of the play. Mark Antony subverts the epideictic genre, by turning it into a potent weapon for shaping political choices. Such effects are also known in real life. During the battle for Irish independence, for example, graveside speeches in praise of dead nationalists were a means of invoking support for the cause they stood for.

Display rhetoric, deliberative rhetoric, or both?

'It has seemed right, before we turn away from this place in which we have laid the mortal remains of O'Donovan Rossa, that one among us should, in the name of all, speak the praise of that valiant man, and endeavour to formulate the thought and the hope that are in us as we stand around his grave. And if there is anything that makes it fitting that I, rather than some other, rather than one of the grey-haired men who were young with him and shared in his labour and in his suffering, should speak here, it is perhaps that I may be taken as speaking on behalf of a new generation that has been re-baptized in the Fenian faith, and that has accepted the responsibility of carrying out the Fenian programme. I propose to you then that, here by the grave of this unrepentant Fenian, we renew our baptismal vows; that, here by the grave of this unconquered and unconquerable man, we ask of God, each one for himself, such unshakable purpose, such high and gallant courage, such unbreakable strength of soul as belonged to O'Donovan Rossa.'

(From Patrick Pearse's eulogy for the (Fenian) Irish nationalist O'Donovan Rossa, 1 August 1915)

Deliberative rhetoric, then, may often appear disguised as something else. US speechwriters have a term for the bland remarks drafted for delivery by the President to visiting delegations of teachers, war veterans, and other minor worthies. They call them 'Rose Garden rubbish', because it is in the White House Rose Garden that this type of event often takes place. Yet along with the expected praise of hardworking teachers and brave veterans—who are perhaps present to receive medals or awards—this type of speech will very often include some more political observations, under an anodyne cloak. Comments to teachers might also justify the President's own educational programme; comments to veterans might be linked with remarks justifying a present day war. Getting too political, however, might be seen by the listeners as a breach of decorum, which was once the cause of Prime Minister Tony Blair being slow-handclapped by the Women's Institute (which is not in general a notoriously tough audience). In short, it may not always be possible to say definitively which branch of oratory a particular speech belongs to. What we can do is look for the forensic, deliberative, or epideictic elements in any particular piece of rhetoric.

The five canons

There are also generally said to be 'five canons' of rhetoric: 1) invention/discovery; 2) arrangement; 3) style; 4) memory; and 5) delivery. This represents a division of rhetoric into different elements, and can apply no matter which branch or branches of oratory a speech belongs to. Invention/discovery refers to the process of coming up with arguments appropriate to the situation. This involves reflecting on the nature of the audience. Say, for example, the subject is healthcare: will the listeners expect a scientific discourse, a partisan policy speech, or 'Rose Garden rubbish' commending healthworkers? The process also involves assembling the necessary evidence. It might be thought that whereas speeches in court cases require evidence,

those made on social occasions do not. In fact, although
the evidence required is of a different kind, it is still needed.
The best man's speech at a wedding contains evidence in
the form of anecdote, generally aimed at demonstrating that the
groom is a lovable rascal whose wild days are now behind him.
If it is not selected and deployed with sufficient care, things can
go embarrassingly wrong.

Where the subject matter of a speech is controversial, invention/
discovery also involves deciding what is really at issue. This may
be a dispute as to the facts or, equally significantly, over the
interpretation of the facts. Mandela agreed with his prosecutors
that he had carried out acts that were forbidden under existing
South African law, but unlike them he denied that this law could
be considered legitimate, given that it was imposed by the white
minority on a majority population that had no say in making it.
Naturally, the authorities refused to accept these as the true terms
of the debate, because to do so would have undermined the basis
on which they asserted their power. Thus, the two parties to a
disagreement may well not agree what it is that they are arguing
about, because accepting the other's definitions will shift the
dispute to potentially losing ground. Hence, if Professor X accuses
Professor Y of plagiarism, she may justify raising the point by
claiming that academic standards are at stake. In response, Y may
accept having made some trivial footnoting errors but refuse the
definition of plagiarism. Rather, she may suggest, X is being
absurdly pedantic: 'This argument is *really* about X's inability to
come to terms with her seething professional jealousy of my
superior work and rapid promotion.' If a politician is accused of
misuse of funds, her opponents may say that the allegations cast
doubt on her fitness for office; she may react by saying that the
charges are 'politically motivated' and 'a distraction from the real
issues in this campaign.'

The technique of *stasis* is a series of standard questions that helps
rhetors decide, within the process of invention/discovery, what they

themselves believe is fundamentally at stake. Take the case of the politician and the questions she may ask herself when preparing a speech in her defence. Did anything happen? (Yes, a few thousand dollars briefly ended up in the wrong account.) Was any harm done? (Yes, there was a technical breach of the rules, which I regret, but I returned the money as soon as it was brought to my attention.) Was the harm done serious? (No, this was a minor infringement that occurred accidentally without any intent to deceive.) Is this the right place to be discussing this? (No, let us wait for the official report into the matter and in the meantime get back to debating the vital questions facing the country.) In working out how to elaborate her answers to these questions, she may also consider the *topoi* or 'topics of invention'—a series of ways of looking at problems in order to generate arguments. For example, considering the *topos* of comparison could help her think of arguing that her errors were much less significant than those committed by her opponents or by past occupants of the office for which she is running. The *topos* of cause and effect could lead her to argue that her mistake was caused by the fact that she was distracted by the pressing issues of the day, but that the results of it were at any rate trivial. Of course, her opponents would likely use the identical techniques to come up with radically different arguments.

The second canon, 'Arrangement', concerns the ordering of material. In the classical period, a rather rigid formula was laid down. This held that there should be an introduction, a narration of the facts, an outline of the structure of the speech, a proof of the argument, a refutation of opposing arguments, and a conclusion (or peroration). It is useful to be aware of this structure when analysing Classical or Renaissance rhetoric, but it should not be imagined that it was invariably followed. Nor does a successful speech necessarily require all these elements, at least not in such a strictly demarcated order.

It is, however, important to be conscious of structure, whether you are preparing a speech yourself or conducting an analysis of someone else's rhetoric. This is because the structure of an argument is intimately related to its capacity to persuade. For example, the purpose of an introduction, in Cicero's words, is to put 'the mind of the auditor into a proper condition to receive the rest of the speech', in other words to get the audience's attention and to start to win them over. This may be a simple matter of saying hello and making a joke; it may be more substantive and arresting, as when the Holocaust survivor Elie Wiesel began his 1999 address on 'The Perils of Indifference' by recalling, in the third person, his liberation from Buchenwald concentration camp fifty-four years earlier to the day. Omitting the introduction, and launching directly into the substance of a speech, risks boring or alienating the audience. Similarly, if a stirring passage suitable for a peroration leads the audience to expect that the speech is coming to an end, but further detailed factual material follows instead, the effect will be anti-climactic. When analysing rhetorical structure, always ask: why has this passage been put here rather than there? What is the intended effect? Could the speech have been arranged better?

'Style' is concerned with language. The choice of words—and of the ways that they are put together as figures of speech— can never be neutral. It can be likened to the choice of weaponry. Some orators claim to have no interest in style, just as some claim to avoid rhetoric. But a 'simple' or 'straightforward' style is still a style, and one that can be presented as a sign of the speaker's down-to-earth character and commitment to popular values. In his novel *A Man of the People*, the Nigerian writer Chinua Achebe presented an imaginary newspaper editorial, written in denunciation of government ministers sacked for standing up against the Prime Minister's inflationary policies:

> Let us now and for all time extract from our body-politic as a
> dentist extracts a stinking tooth all those decadent stooges versed
> in text-book economics and aping the white man's mannerisms

and ways of speaking. We are proud to be Africans. Our true
leaders are not those who are intoxicated with their Oxford,
Cambridge, or Harvard degrees but those who speak the language
of the people.

This shows how arguments about rhetorical style, a seemingly
superficial phenomenon, can touch the nerves of political, social,
and ethnic conflict.

The same is true of 'delivery'—the questions of accent, posture,
gesture, tone of voice, and so forth, that may have a profound
effect on how a speech is received. Style and delivery are of course
closely connected: note how the fictional article links white
'mannerisms' and 'ways of speaking'. But it is by no means the case
that demotic style and delivery always trumps elite sophistication.
In the 1920s, the British Labour Party made a major electoral
breakthrough, and the expanded body of working class MPs, many
of whom were determined to present themselves as the champions
of the poor, shook up the atmosphere of the House of Commons.
The other parties reacted by suggesting that their forthright
methods of delivery were inappropriate. They accused them of
importing to Westminster the technique of the soapbox and the
street corner: the failure to adapt to the more conversational
parliamentary style was presented as a symbol of Labour's alleged
unfitness to govern (Figure 2).

By contrast, the canon of 'memory' is less obviously controversial
but—even in the age of the autocue—more relevant than it may
seem. Classical rhetorical education included techniques for
training the memory. These included visualizing the different
elements of your speech (represented by symbols, such as an
anchor if you needed to refer to a ship) distributed in different
rooms of your house. By mentally tracing your journey between
the rooms you could reconstruct your argument as you spoke. As
Quintilian pointed out,

2. Cartoon from a Conservative Party magazine, 1923, criticizing Labour MPs' rhetorical techniques

a good memory will give us credit for quickness of wit as well, by creating the impression that our words have not been prepared in the seclusion of the study, but are due to the inspiration of the moment [...] [T]he judge admires those words more and fears them less which he does not suspect of having been specially prepared beforehand to outwit him.

The importance of memory to speechmaking, however, concerns more than remembering prepared texts in order to deliver them verbatim. It is useful also to internalize relevant facts and phrases—the building-blocks of arguments, as it were—from which speeches can be created impromptu whenever the situation demands. Or it may simply be necessary to cover the failure of a teleprompter, a situation successfully mastered by President Bill Clinton during one of his early addresses to Congress.

An ability to regurgitate material without the capability to extemporize can lead to failure, as Churchill found out to his cost. He actually had an extremely retentive memory, and as a young politician learnt his speeches by heart. But just a few years into his career as an MP, his mind suddenly went blank at the very end of one of his parliamentary speeches. He stopped mid-sentence, fumbled for his notes, and with a few lame words sat down with his head in his hands. Some observers thought he was having a breakdown. From this point on, Churchill almost always spoke from a written text, leaving little room for improvization or for adjusting his message to his listeners. In the decades before his great World War II broadcasts, he was widely acknowledged as the author of brilliant speeches, but many doubted his ability to persuade audiences rather than merely to entertain them. Given that his technique was eventually so successful, it can hardly be said that he ought to have used another method all along; but most orators are well advised to cultivate their capacity for spontaneous speech. It is widely and rightly held that the essence of debate lies in the ability to take on board and respond to points made by other speakers. The recitation of prepared speeches without the interplay of ideas is a recipe for sterility—and perhaps worse, if democratic representatives do not feel obliged to hear each other's speeches. Writing of his time in the US Senate, Barack Obama noted how senators often give passionate, well-constructed addresses to an almost empty chamber: 'In the world's greatest deliberative body, no one is listening.'

The three appeals

Whether a speech is forensic, epideictic, or deliberative it is bound to involve an appeal to *ēthos*, *pathos*, or *logos* (speaking roughly: character, emotion, or logic, respectively)—the categories identified by Aristotle. It will usually involve more than one of these, or frequently all three. If urging students to sign up to my class on rhetoric I would probably rely most overtly on *logos* ('This course will be interesting and will teach you useful skills'), but in so doing I would surely try to hint that I was a capable teacher, thus appealing to *ēthos*. I might even try a touch of *pathos*, albeit very lightly—I'd probably quote a moving speech that would be studied during the course, rather than, for example, begging the students to enrol in order to help save my career. I would not necessarily be explicit about what I was doing, however. Speakers will sometimes say 'You ought to listen to me because I can be trusted', or 'Let me appeal to your reason', or 'I'm going to ask you to look towards your feelings'. But often they will make their appeals in less obvious ways. I would risk appearing arrogant if I told my prospective students 'You should take my class because I am a good teacher'—however, if I can behave like one during a five-minute presentation, they may be inclined to believe that I will also be effective in the classroom.

At the same time, the boundaries between the appeals can be blurred or ambiguous. A single sentence can invoke more than one at the same time, for example, 'I can tell you from experience [*ēthos*] that it will be in your own best interests [*logos*] to take pity on these poor, suffering people [*pathos*].' And what is presented as *logos* may in fact be some other form of appeal. To a non-American, the concept of 'states' rights' may sound like it would find its place in some dry, constitutional argument. However, during and after the post-World War II Civil Rights era, it was a highly emotive term that could be used to appeal to white Southern voters who feared the imposition of racial desegregation by the federal government. At the same time, those who used it could deny any racist intent. Rhetors, then, may have many motives for disguising the types of appeal they are trying to make.

Thus, appeals need to be decoded, and this is one of the prime tasks of rhetorical analysis. One very useful tool is the concept of the 'implied author', which was coined by the literary scholar Wayne C. Booth but which is applicable beyond the realm of fiction. The question raised by this term is, what does any given text try to say about its author? Irrespective of the 'real character' of the author, which we may or may not know from other evidence, what does the text suggest or imply about the person who wrote it? The real author and the implied author may be very different people (where a ghost-writer is used, whether for speeches or celebrity memoirs, they may literally be different people). The physicist who submits a paper to an academic journal may in everyday life be a jovial, high-spirited sports fanatic. The paper's implied author, though, will likely be a dispassionate individual, single-mindedly committed to the pursuit of scientific excellence. The paper will not, of course, say this: rather, the reader is led to deduce it through the cold, technical language that details the complexity and rigour of the experiment.

In order to understand how these ideas can help with rhetorical analysis, let us consider how President Richard Nixon deployed *ēthos*, *pathos*, and *logos* in one of his most famous speeches, the so-called 'silent majority' broadcast of 3 November 1969. During the Watergate scandal which eventually brought him down, it became clear that Nixon was devious, paranoid, and secretive. This knowledge is not irrelevant to our analysis—Nixon may have been concerned to counter his already established reputation for untrustworthiness—but our first concern is to find the speech's implied author, in other words, the man Nixon was claiming to be.

The central purpose of the speech was to justify America's continued involvement in the Vietnam War in the face of noisy domestic protests. Nixon began by reviewing the history of the conflict, blending *logos* and *ēthos* by presenting himself as a President who—in contrast to his predecessor—was going to speak frankly about the conflict to the American people. He also claimed that whereas ending the war immediately he took office would have been 'a popular and easy course to follow' he had not done so, because 'I had to think of the effect of my decision on the next generation and on the future of peace and freedom in America and in the world.' In other words, he was a caring but hard-headed statesman who would not pander to popular opinion for the sake of short-term popularity. He invoked *pathos* by noting that, 'This week I will have to sign 83 letters to mothers, fathers, wives, and loved ones of men who have given their lives for America in Vietnam.' This also served as a sign of his commitment to finding an honourable ending to the war: 'There is nothing I want more than to see the day come when I do not have to write any of those letters.'

By presenting the Communist North Vietnamese regime as the obstacle to peace, and proclaiming his own willingness to negotiate, Nixon made himself seem both principled and reasonable. In fact, he suggested, his domestic opponents were themselves prolonging the war, because the Viet Cong would only make concessions if confronted with a united, resolute America. And so Nixon appealed directly 'to you, the great silent majority of my fellow Americans' for their support as a patriotic necessity. He cast the very vocality of his opponents as a sign of their unrepresentativeness and lack of national feeling. Nixon's good faith was in reality doubtful, given that he had earlier triggered the widening of the war through the secret bombing of Cambodia. However, the 'implied Nixon' of the speech was honest, direct, and sensitive to the hopes and fears of Middle America. He was a man who spoke not only *to* the great, inarticulate mass of decent Americans, but *for* them.

Ways of saying, ways of seeing

One level of analysis, then, is concerned with what we might call the 'macro' questions of rhetoric: what is the nature of a speech; how is it constructed and delivered; does it play on reason, emotion, or character? Of equal importance, though, are the micro-techniques which, clause by clause and sentence by sentence, advance (or perhaps impede) a rhetor's overall aims. These figures of speech are incredibly various, and there is no need to attempt to master them all, either as a speaker or as a rhetorical analyst. In fact, many of the most important ones are likely to be familiar from other contexts or even used unconsciously in everyday speech. Do I even need to explain to you what I mean by the term 'rhetorical question'? That technique is useful because it allows you to define a problem and then offer your own answer. Equally, alliteration—the use of two or more words beginning with the same letter—is a concept which will already be known to most people, although they may not have considered its power to drive home a memorable message or to achieve a comic effect. In 2004, the future Mayor of London Boris Johnson managed both when he described allegations that he had had an extra-marital affair as 'an inverted pyramid of piffle', although the striking phrase came back to haunt him when it turned out that the claims had been true.

Johnson's words grabbed attention not just because of the way they sounded but because they encouraged his listeners to conjure up a particular mental picture. Much of language is replete with such imagery, albeit often of a less colourful kind. Again, most people will have some awareness of simile and metaphor. Simile, where we say that one thing is *like* another, draws attention to the fact that a comparison is being made. This is sometimes done very explicitly, as in the case of Shakespeare's line 'Shall I compare thee to a summer's day?' Metaphor, where we say that one thing *is* another—time is money, life is a journey, failure is an orphan—can inveigle its way into the consciousness with less fanfare. Metaphors may, of course, be deliberately chosen to make an impression and stir controversy, as in the image of an 'iron curtain' dividing Cold War Europe. Yet they are also present in less ostentatious forms that are rarely noticed because of their very ubiquity. In politics we talk of' 'landslide victories', 'stalking horse candidates', 'muckraking', 'mudslinging', and ideological 'sacred cows'. When discussing economics we talk of 'cutbacks', 'bailouts', 'debt-mountains', and 'pump-priming'. These are all metaphors, as is describing someone as 'heavy-handed' or 'soft-hearted', or saying that you have 'grasped' a plan or 'thrown away' your chances. Such imagery can help speakers to smuggle contentious ideas into their texts under the guise of familiar and everyday language.

Ways of saying reflect and affect ways of seeing. George Lakoff and Mark Johnson suggest that metaphorical concepts are fundamental to our various world-views. Talking about arguments in terms of battle metaphors—in which people put forward 'indefensible' points or 'shoot each other down'—reflect the wider conceptual metaphor ARGUMENT IS WAR. Other such metaphors might include CRIME IS A DISEASE or INFLATION IS AN ENEMY. Looking in a speech for clusters of themed imagery helps uncover the broader outlook of the speaker. As a rhetor, of course, you can tackle the problem the other way round. If your core belief is that BUREAUCRACY STRANGLES INITIATIVE you may consider personifying officialdom as a serpent squeezing the life from struggling businessmen and women. If you think that CAPITALISM IS TYRANNY you may choose to portray it as a brutal, faceless giant, encircling the world with invisible chains.

The artful arrangement of language is not restricted to simile and metaphor, of course. *Tricolon*—the three point list—is a perennially effective technique. Think of the power of the French revolutionary motto 'Liberté, Égalité, Fraternité' or of the phrase 'Life, Liberty, and the pursuit of Happiness' in the US Declaration of Independence. Even the repetition of a single word can be powerful. When asked to name the three most important elements of rhetoric, Demosthenes is said to have put delivery in first, second, and third place. (There were echoes of this in Tony Blair's statement that his three priorities were 'Education, Education, Education.') Equally common and effective is *antithesis* (contrast). A classic example comes from John F. Kennedy's inaugural address: 'Ask not what your country can do for you, ask what you can do for your country.' (Note the repetition of the words in a different order in the successive clauses, making this also an example of *antimetabole*.) These methods will strengthen any speech—more so if they are not simply shoehorned in, but rather flow naturally from the topics of invention. Reflecting on cause and effect, for example, might suggest the following: 'As a result of what we have done today, we can look forward to a brighter tomorrow.' When the basic ideas and language are in place, phrases can be sharpened by techniques such as *anaphora* (the repetition of a word or phrase at the start of different clauses or sentences) or *epiphora/epistrophe* (where the repetition comes at the end). Repetition—whether of words, sounds, phrases, sentences, or ideas—is a crucial rhetorical strategy. The old advice captures a crucial point about how to get a message across: 'Tell them what you're going to tell them; tell them; and then tell them what you've told them.'

Exercise

Find a partner and interview them for five minutes about themselves. Where did they grow up; what are they good at; what are their ambitions? Using the information you have gathered, write a short *encomium* (a speech praising them) and then read it back to the group. Try to make use of as many of the following techniques as you can: alliteration, rhetorical questions, *tricolon*, *antithesis*, simile, and metaphor. If possible, combine some of the techniques with one another—for example, alliteration and contrast: 'Harry was born humble in Humberside; he grew to greatness in Gravesend.' Be as over-the-top as you like!

Telling the people

Rhetors will often tell their audiences what it is that they are doing, will do, or have done. This is known as 'meta-discourse'—the points at which a speech or text explains its own objects, with phrases such as 'I propose to argue that ...' or 'as I have demonstrated ...' This type of remark is very useful in flagging the argument to listeners and readers, preparing them to expect what is coming and alerting them to key messages. Anyone struggling to develop an argument should consider making use of these techniques. Using phrases like 'what I am really trying to say here is ...' can force you towards clarity. (Another good method is *prolepsis* or anticipation, in which you draw attention to likely objections to your own argument, and then rebut them in advance. This acts as a form of 'innoculation' against the points raised by your opponents.) The meta-discourse of a speech also provides vital clues for those who wish to analyse or answer it. However, it can never be taken wholly at face value. A text can never provide a completely accurate account of its own purpose: even the best-intentioned summary will always be imperfect. Equally, some speakers and writers will seek to mislead about what they are doing. A lawyer may well say, 'I shall today prove my client's innocence beyond doubt' even if such a thing is impossible. Sometimes, even, people will say that they are *not* doing things that they clearly are doing. *Paralipsis* is the practice of drawing attention to something whilst pretending to pass over it, as in 'I see no need to dwell on my opponent's drinking problem ...' Language can be used simultaneously to advance an agenda and to cover it up.

This is not to say that audiences will always be taken in. Contradictions and suspect manoeuvres will often be spotted by people without rhetorical training—although such training might help them spot more exactly where the false move came. The concept of the implied author does not mean that a speaker can invent a new persona out of whole cloth each time they appear in public. If the claims they make are not at least roughly congruent

49

with what is known about their opinions and record they are likely to get into trouble. (Nixon fell when the yawning gap between his public and private selves was exposed.) What is more, audiences are unpredictable. They may be drunk, politically hostile, or just plain bored. But just as a speech has an implied author, so it has an implied audience. This is an idealized group to which the speech is supposedly addressed, for example 'you, the great silent majority of my fellow Americans'. A speaker who says 'We are gathered here today to salute fallen heroes' implies that everyone present really is there for that reason, which, in the case of journalists, casual observers, or the caretaker, may not be true. By attributing characteristics to the audience, the orator hopes to turn the actual audience into the envisioned one, to convert the indifferent onlooker into the emotionally committed patriot. This is what we mean when we talk of a speaker 'constructing' an audience in a particular way—it is the attempt to use words to bring reality into line with imagination.

In order to be successful, a speaker need not necessarily have a lot in common with the audience. Indeed, some degree of difference—in terms of additional knowledge or experience—may lend authority to the person on the platform. However, the speaker and the audience do need to share some points of reference. If a physicist addresses non-scientists, she will do well to use simple analogies rather than complex jargon. (And, in fact, physicists often use analogies to explain things to each other too.) At the same time, she has to assume *some* knowledge. The comparison of electric current to water flowing through a pipe depends on the audience knowing what a pipe and water are; ultimately everything has to be explained in terms of something else. Pitching a speech at the right level is one of the orator's most difficult tasks, not least given that those present will have varying levels of familiarity with the topic: assume that your audience needs to have absolutely everything explained and they are likely to feel patronized; assume too much expertise and they will feel confused and resentful. If the relationship between speaker and audience is not to break down—for example, through an insurmountable level of heckling; or by people walking out—then there must be certain informal understandings between them. These partly concern questions of decorum, such as how long the speech will last and whether any interruptions are acceptable. They also concern other shared values. The speaker and the audience may hold polarized positions, but the attempt to win the listeners over must depend on some notion of ideas held in common. These might include freedom, honour, democracy, national pride, or a shared conception of the audience's needs and desires. Of course the audience may not subscribe to any of these, but even the victim begging for mercy must begin by assuming that the oppressor has a better nature or a sense of self-interest that can be appealed to.

Rhetoric, which is dependent on such assumptions, includes many kinds of shorthand which help the audience reach conclusions without everything having to be spelled out—hence the importance of allusion. In 1980, Prime Minister Margaret Thatcher told her party's conference, 'You turn if you want to. The lady's not for turning!' She—or rather her speechwriters—could rely on the delegates and the media spotting the implicit reference to the policy 'U-turn' carried out by her despised predecessor Edward Heath. They might also have spotted the reference to Christopher Fry's play *The Lady's Not for Burning*.

Rhetors may also 'prove' their points without going through all the stages of formal logic, as in, for example, the use of the truncated syllogism. (A syllogism is a form of logical argument.) This device is often referred to as an *enthymeme*, as it is often asserted that Aristotle used this term in this way, but modern scholars dispute that this is what he meant. In order to understand how the device itself works, consider the statement 'Vangelis won the race because he is from Athens.' There is a missing step here—a premise has been left out. The complete argument might run: 'Vangelis won the race because he is from Athens and Athenians are the best athletes in the world.' To an audience of Athenians it does not need to be stated that Athenian athletes are superior. The speaker can guess that this will be understood by the audience who will draw their own conclusions from the incomplete statement, filling the gap from their shared assumptions about Athenian prowess. In Athens, then, the statement will likely raise a cheer. But what if the speaker delivers the line in Sparta? Using different assumptions, the audience may fill the gap in a very different way: 'Vangelis won the race because he is from Athens and Athenians are all cheats.' The reaction will probably be very different! This is fine if the speaker realizes and intended this, but if the assumptions and expectations of speaker and audience are mismatched there will be trouble (see Figure 3).

A good question to ask when analysing rhetoric, then, is this: What is it that the speaker assumes (or implies) that everyone in the room knows or believes? By definition, these are things that are unlikely to be stated explicitly, as they don't need to be. But at the same time, rhetors constantly give out clues: the inclusion of Biblical references implies familiarity with Christian cultural tradition, if not direct knowledge of the Bible itself. Nor is it only language that gives out these hints. Consider the photograph in Figure 4, which is of Martin Luther King's 1963 'I have a dream' speech.

King's career up to this point had shown his command of visual as well as verbal rhetoric. He had come to national prominence in part through his skilful creation of exemplary 'image-events', which brought to worldwide attention the brutality of the Civil Rights movement's opponents. He was never perfectly in control of the process, which required the involvement of the media. This photograph, of course, is not taken from King's viewpoint but from that of a photographer who doubtless selected this image from amongst multiple exposures. We can see, however, how brilliantly King made use of physical space—the steps of the Lincoln Memorial, Washington, DC—to reinforce his verbal message on this occasion. The second line of the speech notes that 'Five score years ago, a great American, in whose symbolic shadow

"Good God! He's giving the white-collar voters' speech to the blue collars."

3. Cartoon by Joseph Farris

we stand today, signed the Emancipation Proclamation.' His surroundings thus allowed King to invoke Lincoln without needing to mention him by name, and to compare the Civil Rights battle to the struggle against slavery. The symbolism of the American flag, King's scholarly/religious style clothing, and his open-handed gesture (anticipating martyrdom as well as implying honesty?) also work to his advantage. The presence of his wife Coretta (below his left hand on the photograph) suggests his character as a family man. Meanwhile, the presence of both still

4. Martin Luther King

and TV cameras remind us that King's message reached multiple audiences far beyond those people physically present on the day, a point that would not have been lost on US policymakers concerned about the impact of segregation on their country's global reputation. The photo, then, illustrates the fact that rhetoric is a physical phenomenon as well as a verbal one, and its impact is affected by the technology used to distribute it. It also shows that the complexities of relating to an audience or audiences go well beyond the mastery of figures of speech.

Visual rhetoric can be found also in the fictional worlds of cinema and television. We see children playing happily, a picture of innocence; then we cut to a figure with an unseen face watching them from a distance. The juxtaposition tells us immediately that something sinister is afoot. At least, it does if we have been trained to read the cues through long experience of watching movies. The same is true of written fiction.

The phrase 'once upon a time' is a rhetorical device that leads us to anticipate a certain kind of story (although some authors may play on that knowledge to subvert our expectations). Figures found in speeches can also be found in novels, for example antithesis. ('It was the best of times, it was the worst of times'—Dickens.) Our familiarity with such techniques conditions how we experience literature and drama, and paying explicit attention to literary rhetoric can enhance our appreciation of them. Fiction can be seen as a rhetorical world, wholly invented but—arguably—as 'real' and 'truthful' (when it is good) as accounts of society that are based on scientific knowledge.

Equally, our learnt or instinctive understanding of narrative conventions is useful in the realm of fact as well as fiction. Effective speeches often make use of narrative to interpret the world to the audience. This can take the form of the resonant anecdote ('As I was on my way here today I met a woman who told me ...') to the elaboration of the speaker's life-time ideological journey. That individual narrative may be in turn presented as symbolic of a broader collective story or national myth. Social scientists who use the tools of 'narrative analysis' do not try to establish whether particular stories are true or false, but rather to show how people use them to articulate their identities and to make sense of their environment. Rhetorical figures can be viewed as constituent parts of these broader interpretative frames.

Conclusion

Understanding 'the scaffolding of rhetoric' is extremely useful, both when crafting rhetoric and when analysing it. Conscious reflection on choice of language not only has the potential to make rhetoric more persuasive but can help avoid unthinking repetition of stereotyped thought-patterns. However, there is no magic formula either for devising rhetoric or for decoding it. The uncertainties of the relationship between speaker and audience mean that the reception of a speech must always remain unpredictable; whereas to a subsequent analyst the hidden assumptions of a text (which may be well understood by immediate listeners in the particular context in which it is given) may never be finally knowable. Nevertheless, there is much scope for creative approaches that, with the help of the various classical categorization tools, use rhetoric as a window into the social worlds that produce it.

Chapter 3
Approaches to rhetoric

There is an amusing and poignant scene in Alfred Hitchcock's classic 1935 film of John Buchan's *The 39 Steps* (Figure 5). The hero, Richard Hannay, is simultaneously wanted for murder and on the run from the mysterious agents of a foreign power. Having temporarily escaped from his pursuers, he finds himself mistaken for a guest speaker at a political meeting. Called to the rostrum—and trying to conceal the fact that he still has a set of handcuffs attached to one wrist—he makes a hesitant start. But when he sees from the platform that his enemies have located him, he launches into an emotive speech. 'I've known what it is to feel lonely and helpless', he confesses, and makes a plea for 'A world where no nation plots against nation' and 'where there is no persecution or hunting down'. As he finishes, the crowd mobs him enthusiastically—just before his foes take him into captivity again.

The joke—and also the drama—rests on a series of double meanings, as when Hannay uses with real feeling a conventional phrase such as 'the cares and anxieties which must always be the lot of a man in my position.' The crowd detect and respond to Hannay's passion, but they also misread it as a successful example of standard electioneering. He has not genuinely won them over: he cannot rely on them to help him if they learn that he is a suspected murderer. He, meanwhile, is both sincere and insincere. He 'means what he

5. 'Ladies and gentlemen, I apologize for my hesitation in rising just now, but I'd entirely failed while listening to the chairman's flattering description of the next speaker to realize he was talking about me.' Richard Hannay (played by Robert Donat) gets himself out of a tight spot in Hitchcock's *The 39 Steps* (1935)

says' and yet he is also trying to hide what he really does mean. His 'true' meaning is known only to himself, to his persecutors waiting in the wings, and—of course—to the audience of the movie.

Understandably enough, some people react negatively to what they see as over-interpretation of seemingly straightforward texts. Words just mean what they say, don't they, so why bother to analyse them? But the example of Hannay's address to the meeting easily shows us the futility of imagining that a given combination of words has a fixed meaning that can be extracted simply by reading the text—or even by breaking it down into the different parts of speech. The whole point about Hannay's speech is that, on the page, it is fairly banal, yet it is both funny and moving if you know his situation. Useful though it is to identify the various appeals and technical devices that a speaker may deploy, these in themselves do not act as the keys to a mechanical code. The purpose of rhetorical analysis is not to 'unlock' a set of words to reveal a meaning that is innate or set in stone but rather—in part—to identify the *social meanings* of particular statements or symbols in given contexts. This may sound rather high-flown but we all have some experience of doing it. After all, ordinary viewers of the film have no trouble decoding the ironies with which Hitchcock presents them, or in seeing that Hannay's words acquire meaning from the circumstances in which they are delivered.

The film scenario ostentatiously draws attention to Hannay's double meanings, but ambiguity can be found in any complex text, and indeed in many simple ones. 'Ambiguity' was helpfully defined by the literary critic William Empson as 'any verbal nuance, however slight, which gives room for alternative reactions to the same piece of language.' However hard we strive for clarity, such nuances creep into our words unavoidably. In the face of this reality, there must always be room for interpretation (this is not to say that all interpretations are equally valid). We cannot, then, see rhetoric as an uncomplicated series of statements about the opinions of its authors—indeed no-one with natural scepticism of lawyers and politicians would think that it could. Nor, though, can we dismiss it as a mere surface phenomenon that overlies—or attempts to cover up—the 'real beliefs' that supposedly lie behind it. At one level, Hannay's rhetoric is disingenuous (he is pretending to be a politician when he isn't one) but at the same time it is an honest and heartfelt presentation of his world-view. It is a classic example of what Quentin Skinner calls 'the various oblique strategies' which a rhetor may 'adopt in order to set out and at the same time to disguise what he means'. Rhetorical analysis demands sensitivity to such strategies. But we must not imagine that such an awareness will allow us to 'see beyond the rhetoric'; the meaning of language cannot be separated from its structure.

59

Intention and interpretation

If rhetoric itself is simultaneously revealing and ambiguous, it is no surprise that the question of how to study it has thrown up many differences of opinion. Nor is it surprising that the champions of different approaches have often talked past each other. There is, to begin with, what we might call the 'rhetoric exposed' school, which concentrates on denouncing perceived abuses of language by contemporary politicians. The patron saint of this school of writing is George Orwell, whose famous essay on 'Politics and the English Language' attacked the 'euphemism, question-begging and sheer cloudy vagueness' that he found in much political speech. For Orwell, lack of clarity was the product of insincerity, and problems would inevitably arise whenever there was 'a gap between one's real and one's declared aims'. Political language, he claimed 'is designed to make lies sound truthful and murder respectable, and to give an appearance of solidity to pure wind.'

Yet it is notable that Orwell, famed advocate of plain speech, actually delivered one of his most powerful political polemics in the form of an extended allegory about a farmyard. In *Animal Farm* there was a clear gap between his real aim (an attack on Stalinism) and his declared one (that he was writing a fairy story); yet he was not insincere. Of course, he intended knowing readers to spot the gap and recognize his purpose. But much as lying is to be deprecated and clarity is to be commended, it should be clear that rhetorical analysis has to do more than spot divergences between real and declared meanings. If such disparities were always to be condemned, we should have to label Orwell himself a hypocrite. In fact, rhetorical ambiguity can have virtues as well as vices. Orwell surely got his message about the Soviet Union across far more effectively in the form of a novel than if he had written a book or a pamphlet straightforwardly 'saying what he meant'. In turn, political speeches as much as poems or fictions can benefit from the kind of 'close reading' pioneered by literary theorists such as Empson and his teacher I. A. Richards.

But what is the purpose of close reading? Is it possible, in fact, to work out what an author intended? Is external evidence admissible, or does a text speak for itself, contextual information being irrelevant? The so-called 'New Critics' of the mid-twentieth century took the latter view. In their essay 'The Intentional Fallacy', W. K. Wimsatt and Monroe C. Beardsley argued that revelations about what an author meant in a work, such as those that might be found in a private diary, were not germane to interpretation. 'If the poet succeeded in doing it, then the poem itself shows what he was trying to do', they wrote. Writing to the poet to ask what was meant by a particular line would be pointless: if the answer could contain the meaning more effectively than the line itself then the poet should have written that instead. Authors, then, are not oracles who can give authoritative interpretations of their own work. Roland Barthes provided an answer on similar lines in his 1967 essay 'The Death of The Author'. Unlike Wimsatt and Beardsley, however, Barthes also denied the possibility of deciphering a text on its own terms to release its 'single "theological" meaning'. This type of thinking has attracted the label poststructuralism. In this analysis, meaning is created by readers, not authors; and, by implication, each response or interpretation is equally worthwhile or credible.

Much of this may seem counterintuitive, but elements of it are helpful when considering rhetoric beyond the realm of literature. Wimsatt and Beardsley's claim that writers or speakers cannot tell us what they meant may seem nonsensical. Yet, whereas rhetors certainly can tell us things that cast valuable light on their words, it is indeed the case that no-one can be considered an infallible guide to their own meaning. Imagine that a politician publicly uses the word Q, a known racial insult. Under fire from the press, she says: 'But I did not mean to be racist. In my home town, Q is a very innocent word, and I had no idea of this other connotation.' We

Exercise

Read the 'Sermon to the Birds' by St. Francis of Assissi (1182–1226) (Figure 6):

'My little sisters, the birds, much bounden are ye unto God, your Creator, and always in every place ought ye to praise Him, for that He hath given you liberty to fly about everywhere, and hath also given you double and triple rainment; moreover He preserved your seed in the ark of Noah, that your race might not perish out of the world; still more are ye beholden to Him for the element of the air which He hath appointed for you; beyond all this, ye sow not, neither do you reap; and God feedeth you, and giveth you the streams and fountains for your drink; the mountains and valleys for your refuge and the high trees whereon to make your nests; and because ye know not how to spin or sow, God clotheth you, you and your children; wherefore your Creator loveth you much, seeing that He hath bestowed on you so many benefits; and therefore, my little sisters, beware of the sin of ingratitude, and study always to give praises unto God.'

(Reproduced in Lewis Copeland, L. W. Lamm and Stephen J. McKenna (eds), *The World's Great Speeches*, 4th edition (Mineola, NY: Dover Publications, 1999), p. 64)

Without first researching St. Francis's life, discuss the following questions:

Is it possible to ascertain St. Francis's meaning and intentions in the sermon purely by analysing the text?

If not, what kinds of external information (e.g. biographical, theological) would help cast light on the issue?

In what sorts of places might such evidence be found, and what problems and opportunities might it present?

62

6. *The Sermon to the Birds*. Detail of the panel of Saint Francis and stories from his life, by the Master of Saint Francis, in the Bardi Chapel in the Church of Santa Croce, Florence

might accept this explanation or we might not, depending on its plausibility and our knowledge of the context. No-one but a blind loyalist, though, would accept that her statement was not racist purely on the grounds that the author of it said so. Equally, Barthes and the poststructuralists were perfectly correct in suggesting that readers impose their own meanings on texts, often far removed, it would seem, from what the people who wrote them actually intended. Whether or not all such interpretations are valid, this proliferation of meanings is a reality that has to be accepted if we are to attempt to gauge the impact of rhetoric in the world at large.

Yet it must also be admitted that the New Critics showed signs of confusion, and that the poststructuralists (at least in the case of Barthes) descended at times into quasi-mysticism about the role of the reader. Wimsatt and Beardsley's argument that a successful text necessarily reveals its own intention is mistaken. Texts may succeed because of contextual information available to the audience which the text itself does not need to supply: unless later or more distant audiences can recover that information they will be at a loss. Readers of *Animal Farm*, if they are to grasp its central message, do need at least a passing familiarity with the early history of the USSR. Without it, they may end up like the fictional teenage diarist Adrian Mole, who was deeply moved by his reading of the book and consequently decided to boycott pork. Thus, external evidence cannot provide a once-and-for-all solution to the problem of what a rhetor intended, but it can suggest lines of enquiry and eliminate others. For although Barthes was right to suggest that readers (or listeners) generate their own meanings, and although these meanings (the question of how a text is received) are in themselves a proper object of study, we cannot treat all such interpretations as equally credible. It may be impossible to pin down Abraham Lincoln's intentions when he gave the Gettysburg Address, and his words are susceptible of many readings, but someone who concluded that the speech was about the Vietnam war rather than the American civil war would simply be wrong.

Yet, paradoxically, even non-credible readings need to be taken seriously. In his 1991 State of the Union address and elsewhere President George H. W. Bush made reference to his hopes for a 'New World Order'. Conspiracy theorists have taken this as evidence of sinister plot to create a totalitarian world government. Although many criticisms of Bush's policies are possible, neither the internal evidence of the speech nor the mass of external evidence surrounding his career and views lend support to the idea that he consciously wished to establish global tyranny. But even though the conspiratorial interpretation is unsustainable, it is nonetheless interesting, because conspiracy theories offer a window into wider cultural anxieties, as they seem to reveal order and design in a world of frightening chaos. Even apparently ridiculous minority interpretations of a given piece of rhetoric, then, cast light on the society in which it was delivered. It is necessary to examine, as far as possible, the totality of responses, as these may help illuminate what a rhetor was attempting. No-one can predict the reaction to their own words with any certainty, but the range of criticisms a speech elicits can at least give a hint of the responses that a speaker was anticipating, hoping for, or trying to avoid.

Doing things with words

When Bush made his 1991 speech, at the time of America's first conflict with Iraq, he was not trying to establish a world government, but he was trying to do something. He was not merely making an observation when he said that 'The world can [...] seize this opportunity to fulfill the long-held promise of a new world order, where brutality will go unrewarded and aggression will meet collective resistance.' Rather, he hoped to advance his goals through the very process of speaking about and defining them. Rhetors do not merely use words to convey information and report their views. They may also, amongst other things, *appeal* to the audience, *claim* its support, or *confront* it with the facts. These are not only words but also actions—all of which are part of the broader act of (attempted) persuasion. They are known as 'speech-acts'.

The father of speech-act theory was the Oxford philosopher J. L. Austin. In a well-known series of lectures, published posthumously as *How To Do Things With Words* (1962), he made a revolutionary contribution to the theory of linguistics. Austin attacked the existing view that statements are necessarily either true or false and that they describe things. He pointed out that a statement such as 'I name this ship the *Queen Elizabeth*' is neither true nor false. Rather—when uttered in tandem with smashing a bottle against the side of a ship—it constitutes the act of naming. Similarly, the statement 'I take this woman to be my lawful wedded wife' is not purely a description of what the speaker is doing. If said during the course of a properly constituted wedding ceremony, it is itself (part of) the act of marrying. As Austin put it, 'When I say, before the registrar or altar, &c., "I do", I am not reporting on a marriage: I am indulging in it.'

At the same time, it is possible for a speaker to *pledge, apologize, praise*, or *concede* without saying 'I pledge', 'I apologize', 'I praise', or 'I concede'. Austin, then, suggested that different types of speech-act could be performed simultaneously through the same utterance. Take the sentence, 'Would you mind being a bit less noisy?' To use Austin's terminology, the *locutionary* act—the surface meaning—is a factual enquiry about whether the other person would mind being a bit less noisy. But we will all recognize it as a *request*, a *demand*, or even an *order* to be less noisy: these are *illocutionary* acts. Finally, the actual effect of the sentence upon its hearer(s)—whether it results in them making less noise or more—is the *perlocutionary* act. Regardless of what was actually intended, it is the results of the utterance that define perlocution.

Rhetors, therefore, often do more than one thing at the same time. Some of these things they intend and others—in many cases—they do not. If I *ask you to consider* whether a victory for my inexperienced and amoral opponent would be good for the welfare of the country, the illocutionary force of what I say is to *urge* you not to vote for her. The perlocutionary result may be either that I *win you over* through my eloquence or that I *alienate* you through my crude attempts at character assassination. Frequently, the locutionary and the illocutionary effects of an utterance may be the same but in some cases this is impossible. I can promise to lower taxes by saying 'I promise to lower taxes' but I cannot insinuate that the Prime Minister is a drunkard by saying 'I insinuate that the Prime Minister is a drunkard'—for insinuation by its very nature takes place without announcing itself. It should be noted, moreover, that there is no way of stating for certain that a particular phrase represents a given speech-act or -acts. 'I bet' can mean 'I bet you' or 'I did bet'—context is essential, and context requires interpretation.

Furthermore the meaning of a phrase depends not only on its context within a sentence, paragraph, speech, or book, but also on the differing ways it may be understood within society as a whole. Quentin Skinner has done much both to integrate speech-act theory into political philosophy and to show how successful interpretation of texts requires an appreciation of the social and political understandings that surround them. Pre-Skinner, there was a strong tendency to treat classic political writings, from Plato to the Enlightenment and beyond, as representing links or stages in a sort of progression towards modern thinking. As such, these works were seen to be of trans-historical importance and thus understandable wholly in their own terms: they spoke to humankind as a whole, not merely to the time-and-space limited audience that was present at the moment of their creation. Skinner rejected the idea of the 'timeless text'. He showed that, using this approach, later interpreters read back their own assumptions into the works of classic authors, anachronistically attributing to them positions that they never could have held. Ignoring context and reception, these scholars arrived at absurd positions. For example, the writings of the philosopher Thomas

Hobbes were presented as the work of a Christian moralist even though, in seventeenth century England, those same writings were thought to be suffused with a dangerous Godlessness. Hobbes's claim that he was no heretic was taken at face value by later scholars regardless of the fact that, as Skinner points out, 'it is inconceivable that anyone in his situation would ever publicly have claimed anything else.'

Only by establishing the ideological and linguistic contexts prevailing when an author was writing, Skinner suggests, is it possible to identify where that author was seeking to breach convention and thus to innovate. (This is just as true of spoken as of written rhetoric.) Speech-act theory helps show how this kind of innovation operates, via words that perform more than one function at the same time. Crucially important are terms which do not merely describe something but convey a value statement about it. These are called evaluative-descriptive terms. To say that someone is 'tall' is only to describe them, but to say that they are 'untidy' both describes them and implies criticism. Thus, the words 'orderly' and 'regimented' might well be used to describe the same phenomenon, but the former evaluates positively and the latter somewhat negatively. However, such meanings are not static. Rhetors can sometimes appropriate evaluative-descriptive terms for their own purposes, and by imposing new meanings can help reframe the debate. Skinner uses the example of capitalists in early modern England, who sought to overcome religiously motivated suspicions of their new commercial enterprises. They did this by describing their activities in language usually used about idealized religious life: 'It was, moreover, plausible to make such an attempt, since there was a certain element of structural similarity—which they eagerly exploited—between the specifically Protestant ideal of individual service and devotion (to God) and the alleged commercial ideals of service (to one's customers) and dedication (to one's work.)' Hence the evolution of a new sense of the word 'religious' to mean dedicated and exacting, as in 'He arrives religiously at the office at 9 o'clock every morning.'

It is not hard to find more recent examples of rhetorical innovators who have used as their starting point the value systems of those who might challenge them. After Tony Blair became Labour Party leader in 1994, he cast his 'New Labour' modernization project—seen on the left as an undesirable compromise with free market economics—as a means of realizing his party's traditional values of solidarity and community through new policies appropriate to a globalized world. Rhetoric always has a 'context of refutation'—the term is Stefan Collini's—that is, a set of arguments that the rhetor is attacking (perhaps implicitly) and seeking to rebut. It also has what we might label a 'context of anticipation'—that is to say, a set of reactions a rhetor may be expecting and either hoping to cultivate or seeking to head off. When orators pepper their speeches with references to history, then, it is not necessarily because they are obsessed with the past. Rather than being stuck in a time-warp, they may be reinterpreting traditions as a means of justifying novel ideological moves.

'[H]owever revolutionary the ideologist concerned may be, he will nevertheless be committed, once he has accepted the need to legitimate his behaviour, to attempting to show that some of the *existing* range of favorable evaluative-descriptive terms can somehow be applied as apt descriptions of his own apparently untoward actions. Every revolutionary is to this extent obliged to march backward into battle. To legitimate his behavior, he is committed to showing that it can be described in such a way that those who currently disapprove of it can somehow be brought to see that they ought to withhold this disapproval after all. And to achieve this end, he has no option but to show that at least some of the terms which his ideological opponents use when they are describing the actions and states of affairs of which they approve can be applied to include and thus legitimate his own untoward behavior.'

(Quentin Skinner, 'Some Problems in the Analysis of Political Thought and Action', *Political Theory*, 2 (1974), 277–303)

> 'Stability in a word's meaning is not something to be assumed,
> but always something to be explained.'
>
> (I. A. Richards, *The Philosophy of Rhetoric* (1936))

In ways such as this, ideological contestation forces the creation
of new ways of arguing and new political languages. Put more
simply, arguing about things forces us to change the ways in
which we argue. We should therefore see rhetoric not merely as a
means by which ideology is expressed but also as a means by
which it is brought into being. Ideas do not come into being
spontaneously but are to some extent generated, or provoked,
by the demands of the processes of rhetoric. These processes
are interactive in that rhetors are to some extent forced to
acknowledge the existence of other points of view—if only to
dismiss them—and to head off objections to their own arguments.
They may have the sensation that they are delivering age-old
truths, but they are often obliged to find new ways of expressing
them. These new ways of expression never leave the ideas
unaltered. It is a natural habit to see ideas as representing content
and language as representing form and as thus being in some
sense separate from, or even antithetical to, one another. Yet
ideologies are themselves rhetorical constructs, that is to say, they
cannot be separated from the rhetorical structures of which they
are composed. As Alan Finlayson and James Martin suggest, 'one
of the things an ideology is, is a *style* of argumentation'. And just
as ideology is embedded in language, so too it is embedded in the
quasi-theatrical, technical and cultural contexts in which
language is delivered.

New Rhetorics

It is the awareness of societal context that distinguishes modern
rhetorical scholarship from its forerunners. In the twentieth
century, believing that the discipline had fallen into decline and

even contempt, a number of theorists proposed the development of a 'new rhetoric'. Such suggestions did not represent a rejection of classically informed rhetoric so much as a desire to broaden, revalue, and revitalize it with new understandings derived, in part, from the new disciplines of social science. In *The Philosophy of Rhetoric* I. A. Richards offered a famous definition: 'Rhetoric, I urge, should be a study of misunderstanding and its remedies.' A key misunderstanding came about, he argued, from what he termed the 'Proper Meaning Superstition'—the idea, encouraged by the old-style rhetoric manuals, that every word has a stable 'true' meaning and that it should always be used in that sense. Efforts to prevent deviation from supposedly correct usage were in fact, Richards suggested, a form of attempted social control. A seemingly innocuous focus on the finer points of expression—and pronunciation—could serve as a tool of social differentiation and hence as a class weapon. But efforts to pin fixed meanings on words were ultimately futile: 'where the old Rhetoric treated ambiguity as a fault in language, and hoped to confine or eliminate it, the new Rhetoric sees it as an inevitable consequence of the powers of language and as an indispensable means of our most important utterances'.

Kenneth Burke, a scholar who had a powerful impact on rhetorical theory, put the contrast in slightly different terms, but also emphasized the shift away from conventional assumptions about the rationality of discourse. 'The key term for the old rhetoric was "persuasion" and its stress was upon deliberate design', he wrote. 'The key term for the "new" rhetoric would be "identification," which can include a partially "unconscious" factor in appeal.' Burke's concept of 'identification' was not, as he acknowledged, completely new: techniques for speakers to identify themselves with their audiences went back at least to Aristotle. He did, however, provide a compelling sociological-cum-psychological explanation for its importance. People are inherently divided from one another but experience a powerful desire to belong. 'If men were not apart from one another, there would be no need for the rhetorician to proclaim their unity', Burke explained; and if their unity (or identification) was genuinely complete there would be no conflict. 'But put identification and division ambiguously together, so that you cannot know for certain just where one ends and the other begins, and you have the characteristic invitation to rhetoric.' This insight can also be put in the language of 'in-groups' and 'out-groups' as developed by social identity theorists. In-groups are those to which we feel we belong, or to which we would like to belong: the cool, the respectable, the elite. Out-groups are those for which we feel distaste or against which we have the urge to compete, and of which we wish to avoid becoming members. Politicians frequently suggest that their party stands for an in-group which embodies almost everyone in the country and that their opponents represent an extreme or contemptible out-group. By identifying themselves with an in-group to which voters might like to think that they belong—that of hardworking, middle class Americans, say—they hope that the voters will in turn identify themselves with the politicians. Hence, there is the almost omnipresent strife over group identity and 'national values' and the constant attempts of politicians to portray their competitors as transgressors against these. For example, in 2011, the 'Occupy Wall Street' protesters cast themselves as the in-group with the slogan, 'We are the 99 per cent'. Their opponents reacted by presenting them as an 'un-American' out-group.

Burke argued that rhetoric is '*rooted in* [...] *the use of language as a symbolic means of inducing cooperation in beings that by nature respond to symbols.*' In his account, figures of speech function as signs that rhetors use to identify—and ingratiate—themselves with the audience. The choice of symbols directs the audience's attention in different ways. In Burke's phraseology, 'terministic screens' are the linguistic filters which cause us to see situations in particular fashions. The building of a factory could be seen as either positive or negative, depending on the framing device used. It could be seen either as contributor to economic growth or an environmental danger. If the factory is to be built in India it could be seen either as a sign of economic development or as a threat to jobs elsewhere. Naturally, we all have instinctive biases. It is unlikely that an Indian's first reaction to a new local factory would be to worry about Western unemployment. But at the same time we can be cued, quite easily, to accept the screen put in front of us. It is notoriously easy to get very different results from opinion polls by varying the question. (For example, one might find high support for military action against another country 'in order to prevent it acquiring nuclear weapons' if this were presented as the sole option but find lower support if other options such as economic sanctions or negotiations were presented too.) Such cues, of course, do not come only from formal rhetoric but also from the products of mass culture: TV, websites, the slogans to be found on mouse-mats and sandwich-wrappers. As one commentator noted, Burke drew as readily on popular films and radio shows as on Sophocles or Shakespeare, as those things too were full of 'symbolic and rhetorical ingredients'.

'Man is the symbol-using animal'

'Take away our books, and what little do we know about history, biography, even something so "down to earth" as the relative position of seas and continents? What is our "reality" for today (beyond the paper-thin line of our own particular lives) but all this clutter of symbols about the past combined with whatever things we know mainly through maps, magazines, newspapers, and the like about the present? In school, as they go from class to class, students turn from one idiom to another. The various courses in the curriculum are in effect but so many different terminologies. And however important to us is the tiny sliver of reality each of us has experienced firsthand, the whole overall "picture" is but a construct of our symbol systems.'

(Kenneth Burke, *Language as Symbolic Action* (1968))

Emphasis on identity and symbolism can also be found in Chaïm Perelman and Lucie Olbrechts-Tyteca's landmark work *The New Rhetoric*. One of the key contributions of the book was to show the importance of epideictic rhetoric, traditionally presented as quite separate from the deliberative form. Epideictic speech should not be seen merely as a form of display by the orator. By praising some values and disparaging others, it 'strengthens the disposition toward action by increasing adherence to the values it lauds' and 'tries to establish a sense of communion centered around particular values recognized by the audience'. The presence of symbols such as flags or crosses helps reinforce such values. As Perelman noted in a later article, the ritual surrounding symbols 'prescribes the conduct to be observed in order to give them the respect they deserve: at a given moment one must rise or kneel, salute or sing in chorus. With respect to these it is improper to pose questions, to raise doubts, to ask for explications, or to rebel.'

Although there has never been a single, monolithic 'new rhetoric', the various New Rhetorics that do exist have in common a desire to locate rhetoric in its social context. Orators are not seen as autonomous agents making rational calculations of how to sway audiences (although that may be what they think that they are doing). Rather, they are afloat upon a sea of shifting meanings, surrounded by the flotsam and jetsam of changing usage. They may influence crowd identity through the manipulation of values that are understood as fixed, but they themselves have absorbed and perhaps distorted these values through selective processes that are at least partly unconscious. To apply these thoughts to one's own situation may create a sense of alienation or disempowerment or of not being in control. 'Do we simply use words, or do they not also use us?' asked Burke.

So, whereas the New Rhetorics provide valuable tools for the critic, they simultaneously undermine the confidence, present in the old-style rhetorical manuals and their modern successors, that it is possible to lay down prescriptions for speaking in the form of inviolable laws. Although there are many aspects of communication that are susceptible to scientific investigation, we cannot hope for an all-encompassing 'science of rhetoric' that would apply irrespective of time and culture. Recent history is littered with politicians who thought that they had a full grasp of modern media techniques only to find themselves a few years later struggling to navigate a hostile press, their charts suddenly out of date. It is now standard to say that such people have 'lost control of the narrative'; but the sense that they had full control of it at any stage was probably an illusion. This is not to say that there is nothing to be gained from mastering rhetorical techniques, even if some of the claims to be found in some of today's guides to them are exaggerated. ('You'll mold the minds of men and women to your will, and make any group yield to your voice', promises one recent book, if only you'll follow its advice.) Such techniques represent valuable survival skills—but they are not a map of the territory in which you'll be using them.

How to conduct a rhetorical analysis?

There has been an enormous amount of work on rhetoric carried out by thinkers who do not necessarily see themselves as rhetorical scholars or as carrying out formal rhetorical analysis. Indeed, part of the stimulus for the New Rhetorics was the perception that rhetorical study had fallen into oblivion and that questions that had formed parts of its concerns had floated away to be treated by other disciplines. Although Departments of Rhetoric proliferate at universities in the United States, there and elsewhere issues surrounding rhetoric are also dealt with within the fields of political science, political psychology, literature, linguistics, discourse analysis, even economics—and the list could go on. For example, it was the evolutionary biologist Richard Dawkins who formulated the idea of the 'meme'—a 'unit of cultural transmission' that spreads ideas rapidly across society via imitative processes. When one considers the phrases and catchwords that, from small beginnings, suddenly become ubiquitous, the relevance of the meme to rhetoric is obvious.

It follows, then, that students of rhetoric need to be open-minded when it comes to selecting their approach. It equally follows that there is little hope of a single individual grasping all the relevant literatures in their entirety, and there can be no shame in an eclecticism that takes inspiration wherever it happens to be found. It further follows that there cannot be any rigid formula for how to conduct a rhetorical analysis (a task which lecturers often set their students). Not only do different texts require different methods, but the question of *how* to analyse should be taken as the starting point for inquiry, not dictated by a teacher or taken as a given. This is cold comfort for those who like to have their work broken down into a prescribed list of baby-steps, but enormously liberating for anyone who is prepared to risk making mistakes in the interests of creativity. What follows, then, is a list of suggestions of various things you might like to try, and some hints at their strengths and drawbacks. It is a guide to some of the tools you might like to use, not a faultless set of instructions for cracking a safe.

First, you need to decide what it is that you're going to analyse. Classical or medieval texts present certain kinds of difficulty, but it should not be assumed that modern or contemporary texts are necessarily 'easier'. You also need to choose whether you are going to examine a single text intensively or to look at a theme over a period of time. Of course, the two approaches are not mutually exclusive. If writing about a speech made by Jawaharlal Nehru, you will need to put it in the context of other speeches he made on similar topics and of Indian nationalist rhetoric more generally. (You might also wish to think about international audiences that Nehru may have been considering too.) It is then necessary to think—in the case of spoken rhetoric—about whether a text exists in a form that accurately represents what was actually said. It is tempting to assume that an 'authentic' text is essential if meaningful analysis is to take place. Yet, where accounts conflict that very fact can lead to pregnant questions. And apparently inauthentic texts can themselves be legitimate objects of study. Cicero rewrote for publication a speech that had failed to secure the acquittal of his client Milo, who was sent into exile. But why should Cicero advertise his failure by circulating the speech, even in an improved form? Aislinn Melchior makes the plausible argument that it was a political act, and that 'Cicero's additions were written and produced with the goal of achieving Milo's eventual pardon and recall.' In other words, the fact that the published version is 'inaccurate' in the common sense of the term does not diminish its value as a source. It may be tempting, nonetheless, to turn away from these complexities by choosing modern speeches which, having been recorded, allow for the possibility of textual verification. But remember: sound and film recordings provide material for another layer of analysis (of tone of voice, gesture, camera-perspective, etc.) that will need to be carried out too. The abundance of evidence can cause as much difficulty as its scarcity!

Having made a choice, however roughly, of the type of material you are going to consider, you need to decide whether you are going to take a primarily qualitative or quantitative approach. So far, we've been looking at things in qualitative terms—the ways that words are used, not how often they are used. Yet even qualitative analysis is bound to include references to quantities at least in general terms. We will want to know if a speaker hammered home the same point again and again, or if they only made it once. We will be interested in the repeated use of similar metaphors; we will want to know if an orator spoke several times a week or only once a year. In the era of the large-scale digitization of texts, quantitative analysis is becoming ever-easier. Consider Figure 7, which shows the relative popularity of the terms 'rhetoric' and 'discourse' as a percentage of the words found within Google's huge corpus of electronic books published in English between 1800 and 2000. (The actual percentages are tiny, but this is true for virtually any word. By way of comparison, the term

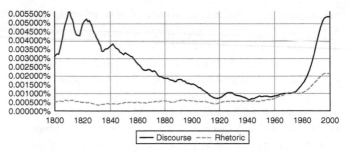

0.005500%
0.005000%
0.004500%
0.004000%
0.003500%
0.003000%
0.002500%
0.002000%
0.001500%
0.001000%
0.000500%
0.000000%

1800 1820 1840 1860 1880 1900 1920 1940 1960 1980 2000

—— Discourse --- Rhetoric

7. Relative popularity of the terms 'discourse' and 'rhetoric'

'food' peaked at around 0.015 per cent during the same period.
Some caution is also required surrounding the quality of the data.)

How can we interpret this information? We can see a clear trend
for the growing popularity of 'rhetoric' from 1960 onwards, and
we could hypothesize that this reflects a revival of the discipline
under the stimulus of the New Rhetorics. Alternatively, the growth
could be accounted for by a growing scepticism about political
language and an increased willingness to dismiss things as 'just
rhetoric'. By contrast, no *prima facie* explanation suggests itself
for why 'discourse' should have declined from its nineteenth
century highs, although it is clear that, at some point, it stopped
being normal to refer to a speech as 'a discourse'. However, it is
plausible to think that the word's 1980s revival was in some way
connected with the rise of postmodernist theory which tends to
use the term a lot. It is evident, then, that its meaning has
changed: Michel Foucault (widely translated into English) did not
use it in the same way as, for example, the eighteenth century
Scottish rhetorician Hugh Blair.

All this points to the fact that as soon as we perform a quantitative
analysis we have to start looking at the results from the qualitative
point of view. If a computer cannot tell the difference between
'sandwich' the food and 'Sandwich' the place, one cannot expect it

to distinguish between nuances of conceptual meaning. It is possible to 'hand-code' texts to determine from context, for example, whether the word 'liberal' is being used politically or in the sense of 'generosity'. But this process is laborious and may be affected by the biases of the coder, and it may be thought that the ability to crunch huge amounts of uncoded data is some compensation for the analytical problems that result. It is possible to do far more than simply count the frequency of particular words or phrases. One can measure the complexity of a speaker's sentences, for instance, or assign scores to words on a left–right ideological spectrum to arrive at an overall score for a particular text. (It is generally necessary to use a corpus of comparable texts, such as US presidents' inaugural addresses or party manifestos, if the results are to be useful.) However, although some political scientists seem to think otherwise, it is impossible to assume that words retain stable meanings across time and cultures. Moreover, left-wingers may succeed in appropriating 'right-wing' words and *vice versa*. Texts, therefore, cannot be treated merely as 'collections of word data' that can be mapped on to 'predefined policy dimensions' in an uncomplicated way. Quantitative analysis of word data can raise some very interesting questions, but it is a complement to the close reading of texts, not a substitute for it.

It may indeed be easiest for the would-be analyst to start with a close reading of a short modern speech, the authenticity of which is not at issue. You may wish to begin by identifying deliberative, forensic, or epideictic elements. Try to spot the way in which different sections make different appeals—to *ēthos*, *pathos*, and *logos*. Flag up any ambiguities. Find examples of imagery. Locate figures of speech and attempt to work out how they advance (or perhaps inhibit) the speaker's message. Above all, try to determine what is really at issue—for example, does an apparently anodyne set of commonplaces disguise an attack on the values of an out-group? Reflect on what other sources of evidence—such as speech drafts, photographs, diary entries or newspapers—could assist your analysis if it were available to you. Having considered

Exercise: debating approaches to rhetorical analysis

Each member of the group should bring with them a text for potential analysis. This could be a political speech or pamphlet, a sermon, a poem, or—why not?—a cereal box. (You could ask: who is the 'implied eater' of this cereal?) The group should then debate which text to choose for analysis. What are the problems and opportunities presented by each? Are there theoretical approaches that would be particularly suited to each text? What kinds of additional evidence would it be desirable to have, and is it likely to be available? Devise a presentation justifying the group's final choice of text and approach.

these things, think about how you can arrange your findings and deliver them in the most effective way possible. Remember that, even if there can never be any definitive 'right' answers when tackling problems such as these, there are at least such things as convincing ones.

Conclusion

The various approaches to rhetoric we have looked at all bring us back, to a greater or lesser extent, to the problem of meaning and intention. That is what seems to fascinate us, although pinning it down is infuriatingly difficult. It is not necessary to be too despondent about the possibility of ever saying anything concrete about a rhetor's intentions. Although it will never be possible to provide an absolute and definitive answer to what a particular book or speech means, it will certainly be possible to narrow the possible range of meanings and to use evidence outside the text to cast light on it. But what the author intended is perhaps less important than we tend to assume. Take St. Francis of Assisi's celebrated 'Sermon to the Birds'. Did he really think that he could talk to birds, or did he actually mean to convey a message to his human listeners, or both? Does the text that we have even remotely resemble anything that he really said? These are undeniably interesting questions, but not perhaps the most interesting ones that we could ask. We could equally raise the issue of why those who circulated (or perhaps even created) the sermon's text apparently found it so important to claim that Francis talked to birds. Did *they* really think that he had communicated with them? And what does this tell us about medieval piety and how it was viewed? There are no firm answers to these questions either. But they do remind us that, if speakers' intentions are often opaque and in the ultimate sense unknowable, their rhetoric can still provide a window to the values of the societies in which they originate.

Chapter 4
Rhetoric in the modern world

According to a contemporary account published in the *New York Times*, Abraham Lincoln's second inaugural address in March 1865 was a badly managed affair. Having taken the oath of office within the Senate Chamber, the President moved to deliver his speech outside the building, but only one door was open through which the crowd could exit:

> the crush was terrible, the stair-cases and corridors became a mass of surging humanity […] Not one in fifty of that immense audience got within hearing distance of the President, on account of this blunder, and very many only got on the ground just as he closed the address, and didn't even see him.

By contrast, Ronald Reagan's first inaugural address in January 1981 was carefully stage-managed. No one had to worry about missing what he said. The speech won 41.8 million American TV viewers—the figure worldwide was of course larger—a record that has never been surpassed. It might seem, then, that public figures have won bigger and bigger audiences even as, in an age of security concerns and slick media control, their direct interaction with the populace has diminished. It has to be remembered, though, that even in Lincoln's case, the listeners who were physically present were by no means the only audience: they were greatly outnumbered by those who would have read his words in the newspapers, not only in the United States but around the world. Not only did the foreign press report and comment on Lincoln's speech, but American papers reported its comments in turn. Radio, film, television, and, latterly, the World Wide Web have of course had major impacts on the way that rhetoric is delivered and received, but orators have been wrestling with the globalization of media culture since the invention of the electric telegraph.

Electronic media and globalization have exacerbated the problem of multiple audiences—which, of course, has existed at least since the handwritten texts of speeches began to be circulated in the ancient world. It is an issue that creates dilemmas for speakers. At British party conferences or American political conventions, political leaders need to present themselves to the national press and television audience as being above mere partisan concerns whilst simultaneously trying to enthuse the party faithful who are in the hall with them and upon whose volunteer efforts they depend for their campaigning. At the same time, a misplaced remark can have international consequences. Even supposedly 'secret' speeches, such as Nikita Khrushchev's 1956 denunciation of his predecessor Stalin, can have repercussions reaching far beyond the immediate listeners. (In fact, Khrushchev probably wanted his speech leaked, although he clearly did not anticipate its long-run effect in undermining communism.) The function of rhetoric under the Soviet dictatorship was of course different from that which it serves in free societies. But the coexistence of, and battles between, democracies and totalitarian systems in the twentieth century gave a new importance to rhetoric in international affairs.

Case study: the rhetorical history of World War II

Examining the part played by rhetoric in World War II helps illustrate how rhetoric intersects with technology and ideology in

John Rettie, the journalist who broke the story in the Western media, describes the circumstances of Khrushchev's 'secret speech'

On the night of 24 February 1956, the windows of the Communist Party's Central Committee building in the heart of Moscow were ablaze with light into the early hours, with the great black limousines of the Party elite parked all round it. This, it seemed to Westerners in Moscow, was very odd. The Twentieth Congress of the Soviet Communist Party (CPSU) had formally ended that afternoon. So why was the Party headquarters still humming with activity that night?

It was not many days before inflammatory rumours began to circulate, fuelled by Western diplomats with good connections to their Central European communist colleagues, and by Western correspondents of communist newspapers. Scarcely credible tales were whispered that Nikita Sergeyevich Khrushchev, First Secretary of the CPSU, had made a sensational speech denouncing Stalin for heinous crimes, including murder and torture. As it was a mere three years since Stalin's death, this seemed barely credible. True, for many months the rigidly controlled press had been full of mounting attacks on the 'cult of personality', obviously a veiled reference to Stalin. This criticism had reached a crescendo during the Twentieth Congress, though only Anastas Mikoyan, Khrushchev's right-hand man, had been authorized to criticize Stalin cautiously by name in a published speech. But overt charges of torture and murder? Surely impossible.

The rumours in 'diplomatic circles' suggested nevertheless that something totally unprecedented really had happened: a furious personal denunciation of the man who, only three years before, had been looked upon as God by the overwhelming majority of the population. Now, it seemed, God had been cast down and showered with accusations of committing appalling crimes and oppression on a massive scale.

(J. Rettie, 'How Khrushchev Leaked his Secret Speech to the World', *History Workshop Journal* 62.1 (2006), pp. 187–193) the modern world. Speechmaking, following on from World War I developments, was an intrinsic part of the global media war that was fought alongside the military campaigns of 1939–45. It had many roles, from establishing the credibility of national leaders and the maintenance of domestic morale, to public international diplomacy over issues such as the demand for 'unconditional surrender', to the attempted legitimization of the Holocaust by Hitler and others. This case study reinforces the importance of taking rhetoric seriously, as something that is fundamental to, rather than a mere adjunct of, the phenomenon of human conflict.

Military historians tend to see the 'red meat' of war leadership as consisting of decisions over troop deployments, the use of secret intelligence, and so forth, rather than at the 'merely presentational' level of rhetoric. This, however, neglects the critical part that leaders' public pronouncements play in modern warfare, as a tool of global diplomacy, as a form of open-source intelligence, and as a means of preparing soldiers for battle and of mobilizing ideology in the battle for moral and psychological advantage. The idea that 'words are weapons' is something of a cliché; it often plays a part in denunciations of modern-day political leaders for their distorted use of language. However, this rarely involves analysis of the mechanisms by which rhetoric is created, delivered, received, and selectively rebroadcast, as a form of communication between both allies and enemies. Even while countries fight they continue to talk to (or at) each other. They do this partly in order to assault each other's morale and boost their own, partly to appeal to (or intimidate) uncommitted powers, and partly to set agendas for the anticipated post-war world. It is necessary to view war rhetoric not simply as a window into ideology or as a means of domestic mobilization (important as these things are) but as a process of dynamic interaction between warring states. During World War II, speechmaking was usually highly planned and consciously targeted and, in the democracies, was often subject to collective discussion beforehand. But, as with all aspects of warfare, finely made calculations could easily go wrong. However skilful the individual speaker, the multiplicity of audiences meant that the consequences of a particular speech could rarely be foreseen; what went down well domestically or with Allies could be disastrous elsewhere, and vice versa. For example, Churchill's warning to neutrals in January 1940 (when he was still minister in charge of the Navy) was popular in France but was greatly resented by the neutrals themselves, who saw it as an attempt by the British to intimidate them. Rhetoric thus should be seen as an important tool of strategy, but as one with inconsistent and unpredictable results.

As a parliamentary democracy with a well-established (if gradually weakening) mass-meeting culture, Britain faced serious challenges in adjusting to the politics of total war. As Prime Minister, Churchill showed gifted oratorical leadership in overcoming these, but it would be wrong to place excessive explanatory power on the talents of one man. In explaining Britain's relative success in the use of rhetorical weapons, we need to consider institutional and technical factors as well as individual genius. Communications capacity, including worldwide radio monitoring facilities and the extensive Empire cable network, helped harvest intelligence from foreign speeches and project British rhetorical messages globally. Careful and efficient civil service vetting helped determine what should and should not be said; there were also new administrative structures such as the Ministry of Information and the Political Warfare Executive. The continued functioning of the House of Commons assisted home morale by providing a rhetorical safety valve for domestic criticism. This was the context for Churchill's speeches, which are often treated as though their sole purpose was to 'inspire the British people'. In fact, that was only one of their functions and it was arguably not the most important. They were a tool of global diplomacy—not least as a means of appealing to public opinion in the United States—and as such were read carefully by neutral governments for clues about Britain's strength and strategy.

8. Cartoon by Stephen Collins. Speeches cannot be understood separately from the technology that is used to deliver and comment on them

The USA was the only major combatant that had to contend with significant domestic opposition to the war in its opening (1939–41) stage, and the only one to hold wartime national elections. There was, of course, a radical shift away from isolationism after the Japanese attack on Pearl Harbor, cemented by Roosevelt's famous 'date that will live in infamy' speech. Even thereafter, however, he was obliged to proceed cautiously in order to balance the sensitivities of home opinion and the strategic demands of his allies. His speeches, like Churchill's, were designed to communicate some types of facts and to conceal others; and, always subject to misrepresentation by enemy propagandists, they were a weapon used by both sides in the battle for psychological advantage. The Americans and the British were highly sensitive to the rhetoric of allies as well as enemies. For example, they examined Stalin's speeches closely, especially as the war drew to a close, in the attempt to discover his post-war aims, when information about the USSR was in short supply. Moreover, the extent of America's own rhetorical power can be gauged from the obsessive German interest in US opinion and their desire to counter it through speeches and other forms of propaganda. The Nazis were concerned about the subversive power of Allied speeches. In 1943, for example, one German paper in Slovakia claimed that after Allied victories 'Jews crowded the streets and squares grinning shamelessly and telling the people about the enemy's broadcasts, manufacturing rumors and spreading every speech made by Roosevelt, Churchill or Stalin.' It seems very doubtful that this was literally true but it does show how much the speeches' impact was simultaneously feared and exploited as an opportunity to promote anti-Semitism.

Although Stalin, unlike Churchill and Roosevelt, had no democracy to answer to, this is not to say that he and his colleagues faced no rhetorical difficulties. The period prior to the German invasion of the USSR in 1941 was a potentially problematic one for Soviet rhetoric, given the difficulty of providing ideologically consistent justifications for the Nazi–Soviet Pact of 1939. However, speeches at this time were carefully tailored to send signals both to Germany and to the worldwide communist movement; and blaming the war on Western imperialism had an immediate resonance in Soviet society.

The Nazi invasion of Russia saw a shift in rhetoric from emphasis on building a socialist society to a more explicit focus on anti-fascism; at a global level, communists now based their appeal on their claims to be leaders in the anti-fascist fight. Moreover, we know that Stalin took rhetorical practice seriously. He wrote his own speeches. Although he rarely addressed his people directly, his pronouncements (including some of his field orders urging resistance to the last) were collected and published. Considerable effort was dedicated to disseminating them in foreign languages. His obsession with the nuances of language reflected a broader Soviet and communist dedication to the power of words, and also a belief that correct linguistic choices had the capacity to shape external reality. The 'Great Patriotic War' came to be cast in nationalist rather than Marxist-Leninist terms—and the military history of the USSR cannot be understood without reference to the Stalinist public rhetoric to which all in society were expected to subscribe.

Words—in combination with spectacle, gesture, and violence—mattered greatly to Hitler's politics. He placed particular importance on the spoken word over the written and, like Stalin, wrote his own speeches. Unlike Stalin, however, he did not have 'the knack of the phrase', and to a considerable extent relied on propaganda minister Josef Goebbels to do his sloganizing. The German people had a hunger to hear from Hitler ('When will the Führer speak?'), as can be seen from their effusive reaction to his halting broadcast after his narrow escape from the 1944 plot against his life. However, it was a clear flaw of his war leadership that, as the war proceeded, he increasingly starved them of his voice. Note the contrast with the 1930s, when European politicians had hung on his words, often desperate to extract from them any hope they could, whilst the Germans themselves were energized and enthused. But, in a state that operated on the principle of 'working towards the Führer', Hitler's speeches remained of crucial importance. So it was with his repeated threats that destruction of the Jews must be the 'necessary consequence' of the war: he was loathe to give direct written orders on such matters, but in this way sent signals to his subordinates to let them know what was expected of them. This point highlights the importance of integrating the history of Nazi rhetoric firmly into the study of the military and genocidal aspects of the German war effort. Rhetoric also revealed the tensions within the regime: for instance, in a 1943 broadcast, Hermann Göring acknowledged weaknesses in the war effort, but he found his remarks censored by Goebbels's ministry when they appeared in the press.

There is a common tendency to see Mussolini as more comical and less threatening than the evil Hitler. Contemporary critics on the Allied side often drew attention to the 'cheek-puffing and chest-swelling' which accompanied Mussolini's 'bellicose roars of Roman conquest'. But although the Western media caricature of his rhetorical style was one of bombast and buffoonery, this was not how Italians viewed Mussolini—nor, in reality, was it how Allied governments viewed him. Yet existing scholarship does not tell us much about the role that speeches played in his war leadership. He claimed: 'my speeches are deeds: either they report them or they announce them'. Here, of course, he was flattering himself as a man of action and, in so doing, playing up to a fascist stereotype. However—as was also the case for other war leaders—there was an element of truth in what he said. Whether he was declaring war, repudiating the Allied demand for unconditional surrender, or justifying the maltreatment of the Jews, his words had the capacity to compel reactions from allies and enemies as well as from his own population. But, as with Hitler, his long silence in the period before his downfall (punctuated by a couple of downbeat speeches in 1942–3) was an obvious sign of his decline as a leader.

In a remark that could have applied to the whole world, the Japanese liberal Kiyosawa Kiyoshi noted in his diary in 1942 that 'Sensitivity towards language is the special characteristic of these times'. The Japanese regime's rhetoric, in fact, presents something of a paradox. On the one hand, there remained the established cultural emphasis on attaining harmonious consensus. This helps explain the opacity and rarity of Emperor Hirohito's public pronouncements, in line with his supposedly divine imperial status. Notoriously, his announcement of surrender in 1945 was couched in the observation that 'the war situation has developed not necessarily to Japan's advantage.' (The Emperor's court style of speech was so mannered that the surrender speech had to be immediately rebroadcast in the vernacular by a radio announcer.) On the other hand, a type of language which presented Hirohito as the head of the national family co-existed with the rhetoric of Japanese technological modernity and a radio propaganda that was crude to the point of vulgarity. As John Dower has shown, such dichotomies were intrinsic to the regime's proposals for the future of East Asia: 'the set phrases that suggested interracial bonding among the peoples of Asia went hand in hand with code words denoting permanent separation and discrimination.' Moreover, the surface ambiguities of Hirohito's position—which subsequently helped him disclaim responsibility for the actions of his subordinates—and his claimed moral authority over the Japanese people influenced American war-time policymakers. In the belief that retaining him as head of state would be a source of post-war stability, they attempted, in the face of widespread US anti-Emperor sentiment, to play down the degree to which he was to blame for the war. At the same time, the American commitment to the rhetoric of 'unconditional surrender' helped create the rationale for the dropping of the atomic bomb. These links between rhetoric and military/political choices reinforce the point that problems surrounding discourse and those connected with decision-making should not be treated in separate analytical compartments.

Hitler's secretary remembers

'On the first of May [1943], National Labour Day, Hitler at last dictated a document to me again, quite a long one. In the old days he had spoken at mass meetings and personally attended celebrations and huge rallies. During the last years of the war, however, Hitler nearly always recorded his speeches, and then they were broadcast on the radio. Often his proclamations were just read out by someone else or published in the press. And he had made no unscripted public speeches since the beginning of the war. "I prefer to improvise," he said, "and I speak best off the cuff, but now that we're at war I have to weigh up every word, because the world will be listening attentively. If some spontaneous impulse leads me into making a remark that doesn't go down well there could be unfortunate complications." It was only on internal occasions, for instance addressing Gauleiters, officers or industrialists, that Hitler spoke without notes.'

(Traudl Junge, *Until the Final Hour: Hitler's Last Secretary* (2003))

Culture, institutions, and technology

It is clear that rhetoric in the modern world cannot be understood separately from the global communications revolution, which warfare (including the cold variety) has done much to advance. At the same time, technological change cannot be seen as an autonomous force, separate from political institutions and culture. If we want to gauge, for example, the impact of Roosevelt's famous 'fireside chats', we will want to know the timing of these broadcasts, how many Americans had access to radios, and how ownership of them was distributed geographically and across social classes and racial groups. Ideally, we will also want to know about listening habits: did people listen at home or in the workplace, individually or collectively? And how did his broadcasts fit in with wider patterns of presidential rhetoric, as dictated (in part) by the structure of the US constitution? Surrounding all technologies are questions about how they are used, and how they are adapted to existing political forms.

Although technology clearly influences rhetorical behaviour, we cannot say that it determines it. The mere availability of a technology does not guarantee that it will be used, and we cannot assume that improved means of dissemination lead, necessarily, to the increased consumption of rhetoric. In the time of Gladstone, the British parliament received more press coverage than it did in the time of Thatcher. Television and radio coverage of major national legislatures was often not introduced until decades after the technical means made it possible. The French National Assembly was first broadcast by radio in 1947, but television coverage did not follow until 1993. The German Bundestag was not televised until 1999, when it relocated to the new capital, Berlin. Televised US Congressional hearings began in 1948—they proved a factor in the downfall of the red-baiting Senator Joseph McCarthy a few years later, by exposing him to the public as a bully—but telecasts of the floor proceedings of the House and the Senate did not begin until 1977 and 1986 respectively. Television coverage of the UK House of Commons began in 1989, but was hedged by rules about what shots could be shown. The cameras could not pan along empty benches, for example, leading to a practice known as 'doughnutting': MPs would sit close to whoever was speaking in order to give viewers the impression that the chamber was packed.

In democracies, it is generally only in such institutional settings that politicians are able to exert such tight control over the audiovisual coverage of their rhetoric. Usually, they are at the mercy of the editing techniques used by television producers to produce arresting news segments. The focus on 'soundbites'—a 1980s term—is a response to this. Politicians have not been exempted from making lengthy speeches, but these are often deliberately constructed with a view to ensuring that particular punchy phrases are reproduced in the TV bulletins. The development of the World Wide Web has modified this dependency somewhat, insofar as full versions of many speeches, statements and press conferences are made available online. Some speakers attempt to use this method to reach voters directly. In 2009, then Prime Minister Gordon Brown delivered an important statement on the issue of MPs' expenses via an online video rather than in the Commons or at a press conference, albeit not with particularly happy results.

Arguably, it is easier for anyone wishing to do so to access politicians' rhetoric today than at any previous time, even if the interaction is electronic rather than face-to-face. Yet it is obvious that, so far, the internet has only supplemented rather than dislodged conventional forms of media packaging. However, the Web does create new opportunities for private citizens to interpret rhetoric and impose new meanings on it. For example, John F. Kennedy said in a speech on 27 April 1961 that 'we are opposed around the world by a monolithic and ruthless conspiracy'. It is obvious from the context that he was talking about global communism. Selectively edited and played over a montage of sinister imagery, though, it can be made to imply that he was warning about a devilish Masonic plot. Once posted online, other users can add comments, suggesting for example that the speech 'got JFK killed', or, alternatively, pointing out that Kennedy himself would have disapproved of the misleading editing.

The media technologies available in most countries are pretty similar, although access to them and forms of usage vary according to levels of economic development. However, rhetorical cultures can be dramatically different. In part, this can be explained by political institutions and structures. A scenario in which the government is drawn from the legislature, such as in the UK, will likely display different characteristics from a US style separation of powers model. But institutions do not explain everything. Audience expectations also play a crucial part. These expectations may be conditioned by formal rules. Yet, for example, the 'Westminster parliamentary model' has played out very differently in different parts of Britain's former Empire. This suggests that rules alone do not determine rhetorical culture; indeed rules are sometimes established by tradition rather than by written authority, and are often interpreted flexibly, depending on circumstance. As Sandra Harris suggests, legislatures can be seen as 'communities of practice', in which newcomers adopt the socio-cultural habits of the institution (including its rhetorical norms) through 'situated learning'.

Even speech outside a legislative environment can be quite tightly circumscribed by rules and informal norms. The first televised American presidential debate took place in 1960; after a hiatus, debates began again in 1976 and have been a feature of political life ever since. In the scramble for advantage, candidates' campaign teams typically haggle over format, timing, and other minutiae. Debates can have a decisive impact on campaigns. Ronald Reagan's performance in his 1980 debate with Jimmy Carter caused his popularity to surge. Equally significant was the exclusion of a third-party candidate, John Anderson, at the behest of the other two contenders, a move that decisively killed off his chances. The debates did eventually become institutionalized, with the creation of the Commission on Presidential Debates in 1987. However, the birth and survival of the debates owed much to contingency and luck. Incumbent candidates tend not to want to debate, as they do not wish to appear on equal terms with their challengers; the fact that neither Kennedy nor Nixon was the incumbent helped facilitate the debates in 1960. In 1976, President Gerald Ford was the incumbent, but he agreed to debate Carter; being 32 points behind in the polls, he felt he had nothing to lose. In other words, rhetorical culture is not fixed, but is shaped by factors that include both chance and the calculation of advantage. Campaign debates have been imitated elsewhere, including in Britain, Ireland, France, and Nigeria, but at different times depending on circumstance. There has been no uniform

Rhetoric in the modern world

effect of technology: the culture and institutions surrounding rhetoric have been malleable.

Like all rhetorical institutions, debates are subject to contestation. That is to say, they are not just places where arguments take place; the debates themselves are argued about as part of broader processes of ideological controversy. In 2004, a report issued by ten campaigning organizations argued that the Commission on Presidential Debates had 'deceptively served the interests of the Republican and Democratic parties at the expense of the American people', by 'obediently' agreeing to the major parties' demands under the guise of being a non-partisan institution. As a result, the report argued,

> Issues the American people want to hear about are often ignored,
> such as free trade and child poverty. And the debates have been
> reduced to a series of glorified bipartisan news conferences, in
> which the Republican and Democratic candidates exchange
> memorized soundbites.

The Commission's supporters of course responded by defending its integrity. But the criticisms do raise important questions about the role of the media in constructing rhetorical extravaganzas that privilege some voices and themes at the expense of others. Some critics, such as the political scientist Murray Edelman, have presented the modern media as collusive in the production of 'political spectacle'. The media is said to construct perceptions of problems in such a way as to shock, titillate, and reassure the public whilst leaving the underlying capitalist power structure intact. It is worth noting, though, that even those politicians who succeed in commanding airtime are often resentful at what they see as the media's habit of corroding—not colluding with—their power and authority. But it is certainly always right to look at debates (formal or otherwise) at least partly in terms of what is *not* being said. Apparently violent disagreements can disguise the fact that the warring opponents have agreed, at least, about what it is important to argue about. This may also reflect a tacit agreement that some things are best left unmentioned or unspoken. Rhetorical analysis, therefore, should consider the seas of silent consensus that may surround islands of volcanic controversy.

The rise of electronic media, moreover, has prompted fears about its powers of manipulation and concerns about public disengagement from politics due to passivity and alienation. Certainly, the mass electoral meeting declined as television rose, although not in strict parallel. Politicians have not necessarily been content, though, with their growing distance from the voters, even while they have been in many ways complicit with an increasingly sanitized and choreographed media process. In the case of Britain, suggests the historian Jon Lawrence, 'many of the traditions associated with election meetings reappeared in new forms' from the late twentieth century onwards. He notes how in the 2005 election, Tony Blair 'actively pursued bruising encounters with real voters in what came to be known as his "masochism strategy", though his preferred venue was the

The classic debate 'zinger': from the 1988 Vice-Presidential debate between Senator Dan Quayle (Republican) and Senator Lloyd Bentsen (Democrat)

QUAYLE: [If called upon] I will be prepared to carry out the responsibilities of the presidency of the United States of America. [...] I have far more experience than many others that sought the office of vice president of this country. I have as much experience in the Congress as Jack Kennedy did when he sought the presidency. I will be prepared to deal with the people in the Bush administration, if that unfortunate event would ever occur.

BENTSEN: Senator, I served with Jack Kennedy, I knew Jack Kennedy, Jack Kennedy was a friend of mine. Senator, you are no Jack Kennedy.

relatively controlled environment of the TV studio, rather than the street.' During the 2011 Irish presidential race, viewers were encouraged to submit questions electronically in advance of one of the candidates' debates. The sponsors claimed to be 'driving electoral debating into the modern age by giving Irish people at home and abroad the opportunity to interact with candidates and participate in a real way in the debate', although, of course, the genuineness of such engagement is open to question.

Lawrence also observes that the belligerent TV interviewer can be seen as a modern proxy for the old-fashioned election meeting heckler. Expectations change, of course. In 1950s Britain, TV interview questions that now look positively deferential were portrayed in the press as aggressive and suspect. Facing competition from the new medium, newspapers had an interest in portraying television in a negative way. The culture surrounding broadcasting is shaped by such rivalries, as well as by the

Exercise: negotiating the rules of debate

The group should devise a debate between two or more candidates. They may be contemporary politicians, historical figures, or invented personae. (They do not necessarily have to be people who would actually engage in a real-life face-to-face debate: try Osama Bin Laden versus George W. Bush, for example.) The group should split up into campaign teams for each candidate. Each team should create a list of demands surrounding debate format that they believe will favour their candidate. These may concern: venue, questions (who will ask them and on what topics?), audience, should the candidates sit or stand, etc. The teams should then negotiate with each other to arrive at a format. Finally, they should present the agreement to the group's moderator (representing the debate commission)—who may either accept it or send it back for renegotiation!

regulatory environment. In the USA, for example, the regime is much less restrictive than in the UK, giving much more scope for overtly partisan programme-making, with consequences for the rhetorical opportunities presented to interviewees.

It may be tempting to see the TV interview as, essentially, an ersatz formula, which allows politicians to remain 'on message' whilst avoiding answering questions properly. Nonetheless, as rhetorical occasions, interviews can be at least as significant as a set piece speech. For example, in 2003, President Jacques Chirac used an interview to indicate his willingness to deploy France's UN veto against the invasion of Iraq. Even when questions are dodged, the answers can be revealing. In late 2011, the Syrian dictator Bashar al-Assad gave an interview to the US journalist Barbara Walters, in which he denied, quite absurdly, responsibility for his regime's violent crackdown on opposition protesters. Although speaking untruthfully, he gave away insights into his self-image and into his strategy for overcoming the dissent. As one commentator pointed out, his decision to address the global media rather than his own people let the cat out of the bag: 'Assad may belittle the importance of international good will—his mantra in the Walters interview was that sabotage from the West and Arab states couldn't overcome the support that he maintained among his own people. His choice of interviewers says differently.' Although modern media technology is often associated—not necessarily wrongly—with manipulation and attempted mind control, these efforts often undermine themselves through the traces and clues they inadvertently leave.

The 'rhetorical presidency' and the 'anti-intellectual presidency'

Much of the academic debate surrounding modern rhetoric has been driven by American scholars and has concerned US politics. The concept of 'the rhetorical presidency', pioneered by Jeffrey Tulis and others, has been particularly influential. The idea does

The rhetoric of advertising

The advertising industry is the ultimate persuasion business. Therefore advertisers need rhetoric, both visual and verbal. The need to be concise imposes major rhetorical challenges but the results can—at least sometimes—be technically brilliant, and adverts form a rich field for rhetorical analysis. Consider the possibilities of—for example—alliteration ('You'll never put a better bit of butter on your knife'), rhetorical questions ('Has it changed your life yet?'), hyperbole ('The Greatest Show on Earth'), innuendo ('Things happen after a Badedas bath'), simile ('A day without orange juice is like a day without sunshine'), paradox ('Hand-built by robots'), and even creative redundancy ('Kills all known germs—Dead!'). The Beatles song 'Being for the Benefit of Mr Kite!', based on a genuine Victorian circus poster, is a delightful testament to the joys of advertising rhetoric.

Of course, advertising rhetoric is deserving of scepticism and suspicion as well. We know that—however much some adverts may present themselves as appeals to logic and reason—advertisers are often trying to implant subconscious messages in order to shape our behaviour without our realizing it. (An awareness of rhetorical technique can help us resist, perhaps.) One might suggest that there is an ethical problem involved in attempting to persuade people to buy things that they don't really need. It could also be argued that the techniques of commercial advertising have infected politics to such an extent that debate has become critically impaired. However, it has to be acknowledged that the critics of capitalism have often adopted (and adapted) these techniques themselves. Naomi Klein's anti-globalization manifesto *No Logo* (1999) became a bestseller at least in part because of the publishers' skilful marketing of its glamorous author and the iconic 'anti-logo' on the book's cover. At the same time, it may be that the rhetoric of capitalist advertising has more going for it than the alternative, if this (perhaps apocryphal) Soviet slogan is anything to go by: 'Toilers in Agriculture! Strengthen the fodder basis of animal husbandry! Raise the production and sale to the state of meat, milk, eggs, wool and other products!'

not refer simply to any and all rhetoric used by a president. Rather it is a critique of the way in which changes in rhetoric reflect (or have even caused) changes in American political institutions. Tulis sees a strong contrast between the nineteenth and twentieth centuries. He argued that whereas earlier presidents had been reticent in their use of oral communication,

> Since the presidencies of Theodore Roosevelt and Woodrow Wilson, popular or mass rhetoric has become a principal tool of presidential governance. [...] Today it is taken for granted that presidents have a *duty* constantly to defend themselves publicly, to promote policy initiatives nationwide, and to inspirit the population.

This was a matter of much constitutional significance and, as far as Tulis was concerned, also for regret. Early presidents, following the model set down by the Founding Fathers, had eschewed demagogic appeals and communicated directly with Congress, generally through written messages, promoting an atmosphere of reasoned deliberation freed from the pressures of popular passion. After 1900, though, the use of the presidency as a 'bully pulpit' (Teddy Roosevelt's phrase) overlaid on the original constitution a 'second constitution' in tension with it and contrary to the understandings of the founders. Presidents began to appeal to the people *over the heads* of Congress in order to get them to put pressure on it. The classic example is that of Wilson, who after World War I toured the country to whip up support for his (ultimately failed) effort to get Congress to ratify US membership of the League of Nations. Tulis believes that, in order to regain some of the strengths of the earlier deliberative model, a revised or rebalanced rhetorical presidency is needed. 'The continual attempts to mobilize the public through the use of personal or charismatic power delegitimizes constitutional or normal authority', he argues, adding: 'The routinization of crisis, endemic to the rhetorical presidency, is accompanied by attempted repetitions of charisma.'

The rhetorical presidency concept has proved both influential and controversial. On the one hand, the validity of the traditional/modern dichotomy has been challenged: earlier presidents may have been more like their successors than Tulis suggests. On the other hand, Tulis and his collaborators have been accused of paying too much attention to policy-focused rhetoric at the expense of other forms and also of viewing rhetoric over-simplistically in terms of crude emotive appeals. Nevertheless, the original idea has proved fertile ground for analysis and refinement. Shawn J. Parry-Giles has suggested that the presidencies of Truman and Eisenhower represented a watershed. In the context of the Cold War, their overt messages to the American people were increasingly supplemented by covert propaganda messages: 'Technological sophistication and classified executive orders increased the available modes of communication capable of servicing the president, expanding the parameters of the rhetorical presidency to include more "hidden hand" communication tactics.'

Bruce E. Gronbeck, for his part, dates the 'electronic presidency' to 1924, the year full radio broadcast coverage of the party conventions began. He argues that 'the electronic presidency is fundamentally different from the presidency as it has operated and been experienced in any other epoch.' If so, the rhetorical presidency phenomenon was not a result of a change in constitutional doctrine but of irreversible technological change. In that case hopes for even the partial revival of the earlier, allegedly more reticent, presidential style look slight indeed.

Perhaps the most important critique of the rhetorical presidency idea is to be found in Elvin T. Lim's *The Anti-Intellectual Presidency*. Lim argues that the problem is not that presidents now speak too much, or to the wrong audiences, but rather that the intellectual quality of their rhetoric has declined at a steady rate. Crucially, he backs up his declinist narrative with hard evidence, making imaginative use of quantitative techniques. One of his key exhibits is his analysis of the complexity of presidential language, using the so-called Flesch Readability formula. This provides a score out of 100 based on a combination of a text's average sentence length and average number of syllables per word: the higher the score, the simpler and more easily readable the text. Calculating the Flesch scores of all presidential annual messages to Congress delivered between 1790 and 2006, Lim finds that, whereas eighteenth and nineteenth century messages were generally in the range 30–50, modern ones score about 60–70. That is, whereas the earlier ones were pitched at a reading level appropriate for a university student, later ones were suitable for pupils around 13–14 years old. Lim also finds a step change in 1913, the year Woodrow Wilson had revived the pre-Jeffersonian habit of delivering presidential messages to Congress orally in person: this represented not a new trend of simplification but the intensification of an earlier one. This represents a challenge to the 'electronic presidency' interpretation, as the trend was in place prior to the advent of radio. Nor has President Obama's supposedly more 'professorial' style reversed the move away from complexity: his 2011 state of the union address, for example, had a Flesch score of 64.4.

Lim acknowledges that a move to simpler language may have its benefits for democratic participation, but argues that 'at some point, rhetorical simplification drives the evaporation of substance', making meaningful deliberation impossible. He buttresses his claims with impressive further evidence, suggesting that presidential rhetoric saw a decline in the use of *logos* and increased resort to inspirational platitudes. He places a considerable part of the blame on speechwriters, whose unanimous preference for simplicity has, he argues, helped operationalize presidents' existing anti-intellectual tendencies. (Judson Welliver, who served presidents Harding and Coolidge in the 1920s, is regarded as the first presidential speechwriter.) Much of his account is compelling. Perhaps inevitably, though, he is (like Tulis) weaker when it comes to remedies. He notes that 'if we demand that presidents infuse their rhetoric with arguments and substance, it will be a lot harder for them to deceive us.' But how are his demands for the elevation and rehabilitation of presidential rhetoric to be put into effect? The apparently inexorable nature of the trends Lim outlines is in fact what makes them depressing. It is perhaps some comfort that *all* ages have seemingly found powerful reasons to lament the decline of rhetoric in their own times.

While Lim's analysis is specifically American, it is likely that such trends are not restricted to the US. The American literature has been pioneering, but a notable weakness has been its lack of sustained cross-cultural comparisons. For example, the creation of a governmental speechwriting establishment was by no means restricted to the USA. The questions this raises about authenticity—does it matter if speakers do not write their own words? Are there implications for democratic governance?—thus apply elsewhere too. At the same time, the special features of the

Exercise: adjusting the complexity of language

Take a 250-word passage of your own writing and calculate its Flesch readability score. (Some word-processing programs have this facility, or you can find tools online.) If the score is over 50, increase the length of the words and sentences so as to reduce the score by ten points or more. If the score is under 50, do the reverse in order to increase the score by the same amount.

American political system lead to rhetorical features that may not be reproduced outside the United States. For example, for decades there has been talk of the 'presidentialization' and 'Americanization' of British politics. In terms of their rhetorical behaviour, this notion has some credibility. Throughout the 1940s and 1950s, prime ministers were quite restrained in terms of how often they spoke outside parliament. By contrast, during a typical month of her premiership (March 1980) Margaret Thatcher gave one lecture, two speeches at party events, one speech at a formal conference dinner in Germany, one joint press conference with the West German chancellor, two TV interviews, two interviews for publication, and made one party-political broadcast as well as three minor sets of remarks to journalists. More recent prime ministers have been similarly frenetic in their efforts to 'go public'. However, there is a significant difference between the 'rhetorical premiership' as practiced recently in Britain and the rhetorical presidency in the United States. A prime minister can only stay in power so long as he or she commands the confidence of the Commons. As the executive is drawn from the legislature, the possibility of office is an inducement to MPs to toe the government line. In the USA, the separation of powers creates a different dynamic. A president may well face a hostile or unbiddable Congress, and cannot hold out the lure of office in the same way. This may well mean trying to generate pressure on law-makers within their own party as well as those of the opposition. Post-1945, prime ministers have not needed to use public opinion in quite this way. A possible exception was Harold Wilson's campaign for a 'Yes' vote in the 1975 referendum on British membership of the European Economic Community, which could be seen as a successful attempt to appeal to public opinion over the heads of a divided Labour Party. Much more work is needed before we fully understand the relationship between technology, institutions, and the form and content of rhetoric. This will require comparative research, which in turn will depend on the revaluation of the discipline of rhetoric in countries outside the

USA. Happily, there have been encouraging signs over the past few years that this is beginning to take place.

Conclusion

According to Walter Ong, human culture moved broadly from its initial 'primary orality', in which the spoken word was everything, to dependence on writing, to the 'secondary orality' of the modern age. This new condition involves new forms of oral communication, such as the telephone, radio, and TV, but a strong connection to script and literacy remains. Newsreaders read; so, most often, do presidents; they are generally able to improvise too, but without writing they would be lost. There was of course a time when newspapers would be read aloud; but the significance of the electronic media lies in their enhanced capacity to forge communities of identity amongst individuals and groups who have never come into direct contact with one another. This is the distinct feature of modern rhetoric, although we must be careful about making too sharp a contrast between the old era and the new. As Ong notes, 'residual primary orality, literacy, and secondary orality are interacting vigorously with one another in confusing complex patterns in our secondarily oral world.' It is clear, though, that the fact that speeches can potentially be viewed by billions rather than thousands of people takes rhetoric into a new dimension, qualitatively as well as quantitatively.

It is hardly surprising that these new developments have provoked anxiety. Concerns about the 'dumbing down' of rhetoric, in which emotion trumps reason in ever-shorter soundbites, and fears of psychological manipulation, cannot be easily dismissed. When public figures so often mouth platitudes written for them by others for delivery at events designed especially for media consumption, it is unsurprising that many people detect an Alice-in-Wonderland quality in 'hyper-real' modern politics. Undeniably, repressive regimes have used, and continue to use, the control of language to sinister and tragic effect. Yet while the 'confusing complex patterns' of secondary orality add to its alienating quality, they also generate a capriciousness that provides an odd form of comfort. In his analysis of late-Soviet culture, Alexei Yurchak observes how the regime's efforts to reproduce official discourse through speeches, slogans and rituals were apparently hegemonic. In the end, however, 'the performative reproduction of the form of rituals and speech-acts actually *enabled* the emergence of diverse, multiple, and unpredictable meanings in everyday life', including those that diverged from the official line. No one expected the system to collapse; but when it did somehow no one seemed surprised either; hence the pregnant title of Yurchak's book, *Everything Was Forever, Until It Was No More*. Likewise, the conditions of rhetorical modernity now seem inescapable, but one day we will be thrown into a new reality, and everyone will think the change was inevitable.

Conclusion

This book has had two themes, which are to some extent in conflict with each other. The first is about empowerment. I have suggested that you can improve your communication skills through attention to simple rhetorical techniques that have proved effective for thousands of years. This is the standard claim of rhetorical handbooks and, so far as it goes, it is certainly true. Although I do not mean to bemoan the current condition of rhetoric, there is today, as in every age, plenty of poorly presented dross. With a little effort, it is not hard to rise above the crowd. Speaking clearly at a sensible pace will likely mark you out, even before you start deploying tricolon and antithesis. Conscious attention to the construction of arguments can improve essays, reports, and presentations to a striking degree: identifying what is really at issue is the first and most crucial step. Understanding rhetoric is empowering in another way too. An awareness of rhetorical technique helps people to assess the validity of arguments and to avoid being misled by plausible but flawed appeals. It can also provide tools that will help counter them.

Yet my second purpose does not provide the same possibilities of uplift. I have shown that rhetoric cannot simply be reduced to a checklist of time-honoured methods which together will turn you into a compelling orator. There are real gains to be made from a grasp of classical rhetorical knowledge. But although technical excellence can make you *more* persuasive, it cannot work miracles. There is no combination of techniques that can be expected to win an audience to your side infallibly, even if your case is logically as well as presentationally superb. I have argued that rhetoric is a social phenomenon, and that its reception depends on the norms in operation in the society in which it is delivered. Yet it is also inherently unpredictable, and even a deep appreciation of the relevant social codes cannot guarantee that a rhetor's words will be well-received. This is especially true in the case of multiple audiences. However good the effect on the immediate listeners, it is impossible to tell how a speech will travel and with what effects, not least given that the media have their own interests. This part of my argument, then, points to the limits of empowerment. Whereas it might be nice to think that there are rules that will help us win all our arguments, that is clearly impossible. In the familiar micro-environment of the classroom or the village hall it may be reasonably easy to calculate the likely impact of our words. But however capable we are there, if we transfer to a national or global stage, we will quite likely find ourselves at sea, although perhaps initially with the sensation of being in control.

That may not seem a very encouraging thought, but it does have its consolations. In the early Cold War era, some psychologists had considerable faith that science would eventually be able to foretell with precision how human minds could be persuaded. For example, Joseph Klapper and Leo Lowenthal suggested as an ideal goal a world in which

> The psychological warrior would need only to stipulate to the researcher the effects he desired, and the researcher, now a mere technician, would need only to work out the mathematics to stipulate in turn the requisite content that should be disseminated over specific media to specific people in order to achieve the desired effects.

Such a model now looks both too mechanistic and not a little frightening. The downside of rhetoric's unpredictability is that we can never be certain of the consequences of what we say. The upside is that even powerful governments and corporations cannot be sure either, and therefore cannot devise assured and lasting formulae for manipulating our minds as they might wish.

Rather than providing a paean to rhetoric as a means of self-improvement, then, I have tried to provide a realistic assessment of its strengths and limits. Yet, I feel no need to restrain my enthusiasm when I write of the force of rhetoric as a tool of analysis. Although it is not a tool that can provide ultimate answers to questions of meaning, it provides a powerful method for investigating past and present societies. As I have shown, arguments about *how* we should argue, which are ostensibly about the surface question of presentation, actually get to the heart of a society's values. Debates about correct bearing and language, far from being trivial, provide 'core samples' of wider debates about behaviour, with class and gender issues usually at the centre. Henry James did not exaggerate when he wrote that 'All life [...] comes back to the question of our speech, the medium through which we communicate with each other; for all life comes back to the question of our relations with one another.' If we want to understand a society's politics, economics, sociology, psychology, or morality, then there is no better way to start than looking at the way it talks about those things—and, in particular, the way it talks about the way those things ought to be talked about.

That is not to say that there is a single sure-fire methodology that ought to be applied in every situation. Classicists and medievalists are obliged to be extremely ingenious in finding new ways to interpret limited evidence. Scholars of the modern and contemporary period, by contrast, often find themselves swimming in information. It is often possible for them to draw a very detailed contextual picture of specific rhetorical episodes. This is not to say, though, that their methods are 'better' or that final answers are to be discovered via the progressive accumulation of detail. The context of a speech will always have a further context, and that context will have another one, ad infinitum. There cannot be a 'totalizing' or 'ultimate' method of rhetorical analysis, any more than there can be a comprehensive 'science of rhetoric'. But although all explanations must leave open the possibility of further questions, it is the analytical journey that matters, not the ever-deferred nature of the arrival.

Moreover, rhetorical analysis is not merely about the static analysis of more or less stable societies. The most important thing about rhetoric, in my view, is its dynamic quality. Although it is often designed with the purpose of maintaining the existing order, rhetoric is a motor that drives forward societal change, and not something that simply reflects it. In any rhetorical encounter, the act of denying something itself inevitably places in the mind of the listener the thought that it may, after all, be true. (Think of Nixon's celebrated remark, 'I am not a crook'.) Likewise, a positive assertion summons up the possibility of its opposite. Therefore, a claim that the existing state of affairs is desirable and permanent necessarily implants the thought, if only deep in the subconscious, that it is undesirable and impermanent. In this way, rhetoric is inherently self-undermining, and must constantly be renewed to face new threats. The rhetorical process is a permanent cycle of creative destruction. It breaks down and recycles arguments which, however much they may appeal to history, are never quite the same in their new form as in the old. The innovator summons up the values of the past to legitimate novel and suspect behaviour; the conservative is forced to change everything in order that everything can remain the same.

Ideas, furthermore, cannot be separated from the language structures of which they are a part. Although the wish is often expressed, it is futile to hope that we can drain away the 'rhetoric' to find the 'substance' that supposedly lies beneath language's deceptive surface. This is not a pessimistic conclusion, but neither should it lead to an over-optimistic view of rhetoric and its potential. The study of rhetoric will not turn us into magical persuaders who can walk on water—but it may at least help us learn to swim.

Exercise

Conduct a rhetorical analysis of this book.

Further reading

Chapter 1: From the Greeks to Gladstone

Aristotle, *Rhetoric*, in Jonathan Barnes (ed.), *The Complete Works of Aristotle*, Vol. II (Princeton, NJ: Princeton University Press, 1984)

William Dominik and Jon Hall (eds), *A Companion to Roman Rhetoric* (Oxford: Blackwell, 2007)

Thomas Elyot, *The book named the Governor*, 1531: A facsimile (Menston: Scolar Press, 1970)

Margaret Fell, *Women's Speaking Justified* (1666) http://www.qhpress.org/texts/fell.html

Xing Lu, *Rhetoric in Ancient China Fifth to Third Century BCE: A Comparison with Classical Greek Rhetoric* (Columbia, SC: South Carolina University Press, 1998)

Peter Mack, *A History of Renaissance Rhetoric 1380-1620* (Oxford: Oxford University Press, 2011)

Niccolò Machiavelli, *The Prince* (Harmondsworth: Penguin Books, 1961)

Joseph S. Meisel, *Public Speech and the Culture of Public Life in the Age of Gladstone* (New York: Columbia University Press, 2002)

John Milton, *Paradise Lost* 1663 (London: Penguin, 2000)

Andrew W. Robertson, *The Language of Democracy: Political Rhetoric in the United States and Britain, 1790–1900* (Charlottesville, NC: University of Virginia Press, 2005)

Quentin Skinner, *Reason and Rhetoric in the Philosophy of Hobbes* (Cambridge: Cambridge University Press, 1996)

Alexis de Tocqueville, *Democracy in America* 1835–40 (London: David Campbell, 1994)

Brian Vickers, *In Defence of Rhetoric* (Oxford: Clarendon Press, 1998)

Thomas Wilson, *Arte of Rhetorique 1554*. Edited by Thomas J. Derrick (New York: Garland Publishing, 1982)

Ian Worthington, *A Companion to Greek Rhetoric* (Oxford: Blackwell, 2007)

Chapter 2: The scaffolding of rhetoric

Chinua Achebe, *A Man of the People* (London: Heinemann, 1966)

Max Atkinson, *Lend Me Your Ears: All You Need to Know About Making Speeches and Presentations* (London: Vermillion, 2004)

Cicero, *De Inventione: De Optime Genre Oratorum: Topica* (London: William Heinemann Ltd., 1949)

Jay Heinrichs, *Winning Arguments: From Aristotle to Obama—Everything You Need to Know About the Art of Persuasion* (London: Penguin, 2010)

Sam Leith, *You Talkin' To Me? Rhetoric from Aristotle to Obama* (London: Profile, 2011)

Thomas O. Sloane (ed.), *Encyclopedia of Rhetoric* (New York: Oxford University Press, 2001)

Chapter 3: Approaches to rhetoric

J. L. Austin, *How To Do Things With Words* (Oxford: Oxford University Press, 1962)

Roland Barthes, *Image, Music, Text* (London: Fontana, 1977)

Kenneth Burke, 'Rhetoric—Old and New', *The Journal of General Education* 5 (1951), pp. 202–9

Kenneth Burke, *A Rhetoric of Motives* (Berkeley, CA: University of California Press, 1969)

William Empson, *Seven Types of Ambiguity* (London: Penguin Books, 1995)

Alan Finlayson and James Martin, ' "It Ain't What You Say…": British Political Studies and the Analysis of Speech and Rhetoric', *British Politics* 3 (2008), pp. 445–64

Marie Hochmuth, 'Kenneth Burke and the "New Rhetoric"', *Quarterly Journal of Speech* 38 (1952), pp. 133–44

George Lakoff and Mark Johnson, *Metaphors We Live By* (London: University of Chicago Press, 1980)

Michael Laver, Kenneth Benoit, and John Garry, 'Extracting Policy Positions from Political Texts Using Words as Data', *American Political Science Review* 97 (2003), pp. 311–33

Chaïm Perelman, 'Rhetoric and Politics', *Philosophy & Rhetoric* 3 (1984), pp. 129–34

Chaïm Perelman and L. Olbrechts-Tyteca, *The New Rhetoric: A Treatise on Argumentation* (Notre Dame, IN: University of Notre Dame Press, 1969)

I. A. Richards, *The Philosophy of Rhetoric* (Oxford: Oxford University Press, 1965)

Quentin Skinner, 'Meaning and Understanding in the History of Ideas', *History and Theory* viii (1969), pp. 3–53

Quentin Skinner, 'Some Problems in the Analysis of Political Thought and Action', *Political Theory* 2 (August 1974), pp. 277–303

W. K. Wimsatt, *The Verbal Icon: Studies in the Meaning of Poetry* (Lexington, KY: University of Kentucky Press, 1954)

Chapter 4: Rhetoric in the modern world

Jonathan Charteris-Black, *Politicians and Rhetoric: The Persuasive Power of Metaphor* (London: Palgrave, 2004)

Victor Klemperer, *The Language of the Third Reich: LTI—Lingua Tertii Imperii: A Philologist's Notebook* (London: Athlone Press, 2000)

Jon Lawrence, *Electing Our Masters: The Hustings in British Politics from Hogarth to Blair* (Oxford: Oxford University Press, 2009)

Elvin T. Lim, *The Anti-Intellectual Presidency: The Decline of Presidential Rhetoric from George Washington to George W. Bush* (Oxford: Oxford University Press, 2008)

Martin J. Medhurst (ed.), *Beyond the Rhetorical Presidency* (College Station, TX: Texas A&M University Press, 1996)

Shawn J. Parry-Giles, *The Rhetorical Presidency, Propaganda, and the Cold War, 1945–1955* (Westport, CT: Praeger, 2002)

Richard Toye, 'The Rhetorical Premiership: A New Perspective on Prime Ministerial Power Since 1945', *Parliamentary History* 30 (2011), pp. 175–92

Richard Toye, *The Roar of the Lion: The Making of Winston Churchill's World War II Speeches* (Oxford: Oxford University Press, forthcoming)

Jeffrey K. Tulis, *The Rhetorical Presidency* (Princeton, NJ: Princeton University Press, 1987)

Websites

Silva Rhetoricae: The Forest of Rhetoric <http://rhetoric.byu.edu/>
*This award-winning site is the work of Gideon Burton of Brigham
Young University. It provides definitions of rhetorical terms and is
an invaluable resource for beginners and experts alike*
American Rhetoric <http://www.americanrhetoric.com/>
*An online speech-bank of American oratory including—where
possible—video and audio in addition to full texts*
British Political Speech <http://www.britishpoliticalspeech.org>
*An online archive which holds texts of speeches given by British party
leaders dating back to 1895*

Index

ONLINE CATALOGUE
A Very Short Introduction

Our online catalogue is designed to make it easy to find your ideal Very Short Introduction. View the entire collection by subject area, watch author videos, read sample chapters, and download reading guides.

http://fds.oup.com/www.oup.co.uk/general/vsi/index.html

SOCIAL MEDIA
Very Short Introduction

Join our community
www.oup.com/vsi

- Join us online at the official Very Short Introductions **Facebook** page.
- Access the thoughts and musings of our authors with our online **blog**.
- Sign up for our monthly **e-newsletter** to receive information on all new titles publishing that month.
- Browse the full range of Very Short Introductions online.
- Read **extracts** from the Introductions for free.
- Visit our library of **Reading Guides**. These guides, written by our expert authors will help you to question again, why you think what you think.
- If you are a teacher or lecturer you can order inspection copies quickly and simply via our website.